The Novel Sentence

*Creative Writing Hints
from the Prose*

HIGH SCHOOL EDITION

By Robert Goodspeed

Goodspeed Publications
P.O. Box 31573
St. Louis, Missouri 63131

Permission to Reprint Copyright Material:

Excerpts from _Light in August_ by William Faulkner, copyright 1932 and renewed 1960 by William Faulkner, reprinted by permission of Random House Inc.

Excerpts from _Orient Express_ by Graham Greene, copyright 1933 and renewed 1961 by Graham Greene, reprinted by permission of Penguin Books USA Inc.

Published by Goodspeed Publications, P.O. Box 31573, St. Louis, Missouri 63131.

Copyright 1995 Robert C. Goodspeed

PRINTED IN THE UNTED STATES OF AMERICA
BRYAN PRINTING COMPANY, PRINTERS AND LITHOGRAPHERS
ST. LOUIS MISSOURI
ISBN 0-9637355-1-9

PREFACE

See that book on the shelf?
Does it wink and beckon?
Open it and read a bit.
Do people, places, and dialogue ring true?
Does it grab and hold your attention?

Then it's a book to improve <u>your</u> fiction and it's probably in <u>*The Novel Sentence*</u>, the motto of which is "Good readers make good writers."

As you read quotations and work in this book, keep in mind Ken Kesey's words on page 65 of <u>*One Flew Over the Cuckoo's Nest:*</u> "Man, when you lose your laugh you lose your <u>footing</u>."

Robert Goodspeed
St. Louis, Missouri

i

TABLE OF CONTENTS

CHAPTER 1. PORTRAIT SKETCHES

Hair and features show;
Choose a portrait from a pro.

Choose a couple of exercises and write 30-70 words each.
Check out the study hints for this chapter (page six).

(1)

Show one countenance with detail lacking;
The other face has had a whacking!

My Antonia

I can see them now, exactly as they looked, working about the table in the lamplight: Jake with his heavy features, so rudely moulded that his face seemed, somehow, unfinished; Otto with his half-ear and the savage scar that make his upper lip curl so ferociously under his twisted moustache. (p. 70)

> Compare faces of two individuals - working, standing, sitting, etc.

(2)

By what criteria is he classified,
General shape or glassy eyed?

Billy Budd

He recognized him by his general cut and build, more than by his round freckled face and glassy eyes of pale blue, veiled with lashes all but white. (p. 52)

> Describe a person first outlined at a distance or in poor light, then close up.

(3)

Ethan, Ethan, late once more,
Can't find the key hid by the door.
His wife responds to long knocking.
Her plain appearance quite shocking!

Ethan Frome

*Against the dark background of the kitchen she stood up tall and angular,
one hand drawing a quilted counterpane to her flat breast, while the other
held a lamp. The light, on a level with her chin, drew out of the darkness her
puckered throat and the projecting wrist of the hand that clutched the quilt,
and deepened fantastically the hollows and prominences of her high-boned
face under its ring of crimping-pins. (p. 52)*

Show someone part in light, part in shadow.

(4)

What occurs the following evening?
Cousin Mattie the lamp is bringing.
She is in the wife's position,
But the appearance...what a transition!

Ethan Frome

*She stood just as Zeena had stood, a lifted lamp in her hand, against the
black background of the kitchen. She held the light at the same level, and it
drew out with the same distinctness her slim young throat and the brown
wrist no bigger than a child's. Then, striking upward, it threw a lustrous
fleck on her lips, edged her eyes with velvet shade, and laid a milky whiteness above the black curve of her brows. (p. 81)*

Describe first one person, then another, in the same
circumstances.

(5)

There is a woman, burdened and blue,
Who works and works - her feelings show through.

Silas Marner

She was a "comfortable woman" - good-looking, fresh-complexioned, having her lips always slightly screwed, as if she felt herself in a sick-room with a doctor or the clergyman present. But she was never whimpering; no one had seen her shed tears; she was simply grave and inclined to shake her head and sigh, almost imperceptibly, like a funereal mourner who is not a relation. (p. 101)

> Describe the face of a constantly worried student, teacher, or parent.

(6)

Grandma's not happy, really what's up?
Grandson, look out, she's about to blow up!

Black Boy

The sagging flesh of her face quivered; her eyes, large, dark, deep-set, wide apart, glared at me. Her lips narrowed to a line. Her high forehead wrinkled. When she was angry her eyelids drooped halfway down over her pupils, giving her a baleful aspect. (p. 48)

> Describe grandmother's face during a moment of delight.

(7)

Divide a face into four or so sections,
Wait for the writer to give you directions.
The aging process is such a pity,
Especially the place that is wrinkle city!

Green Mansions

A curious face had this old man, which looked as if youth and age had made it a battling ground. His forehead was smooth, except for two parallel lines in the middle running its entire length, dividing it in zones; his arched eyebrows were black as ink, and his small black eyes were bright and cunning, like the eyes of some wild carnivorous animal. In this part of his face youth had held its own, especially in his eyes, which looked young and lively. But lower down age had conquered, scribbling his skin all over with wrinkles, while moustache and beard were white as thistle-down. (p. 75)

Describe a face aging in an interesting way.

(8)

Canceling the wedding was an insult,
And Jane will not be his spouse.
In his heart is fiery tumult.
He glares at the manor house!

Jane Eyre

Lifting his eye to its battlements, he cast over them a glare such as I never saw before or since. Pain, shame, ire - impatience, disgust, detestation - seemed momentarily to hold a quivering conflict in the large pupil dilating under his ebon eyebrows. (p. 163)

Describe the side view of someone at a game, shouting.

(9)

A young man of visage open and clear,
Covered all over with shadows or cheer.

Heart of Darkness

A beardless, boyish face, very fair, no features to speak of, nose peeling, little blue eyes, smiles and frowns chasing each other over that open countenance like sunshine and shadow on a wind-swept plain. (p. 126)

Describe a face alternating between smiles and frowns.

(10)

Ready to climb the towering tree,
Delighted, buoyant, very carefree,
He fools and clowns, ever in jest,
Athletic person, always the best.

A Separate Peace

"...what I like is that it's such a cinch!" He opened his green eyes wider and gave us his maniac look, and only the smirk on his wide mouth with its droll, slightly protruding upper lip reassured us that he wasn't completely goofy. (p. 6)

Describe someone making a crazy face.

STUDY HINTS

Do your own work. Remember, you have personal ideas
to put down and so does everyone else. Above all, do not
borrow from a quoted passage.

Before you start, think through these words:

Nouns	Verbs	Adjectives	Adverbs
background	clothe	bony	alertly
color	crown	curved	eagerly
introduction	etch	narrow	forcefully
lighting	frown	patient	joyfully
silhouette	glance	stony	openly
skin	smile	strange	solemnly
profile	sneer	twisted	strikingly

While working, turn to dictionaries for exact meanings
and search in a synonym dictionary (thesaurus) for better
words.

Before reading your finished product aloud, rehearse it
until it sounds good. Read the way you talk only a bit slower
and louder, remembering to pause between groups of ideas so
everyone will "get it."

Begin most sentences low and smoothly raise the pitch to
hit each word expressing a new idea. Practice reading this
while moving your lips: "When you frown, your eyes are dull,
but when you smile, they sparkle."

"Good readers make good writers."

CHAPTER 2. TALK TIPS

Nervous words or dialogue droll,
When faces talk, it's time to roll!

Accept a couple of tasks and write 30-70 words each.
Check out the study hints for this chapter (page twelve).

(1)
When attention drifts, what to do?
Speed up, slow down, yell, or ah-choo!

Of Mice and Men

And then her words tumbled out in a passion of communication, as though she hurried before her listener could be taken away. (p. 88)

Describe someone trying to hold the attention of an officer writing up a traffic ticket.

(2)
When unburdened hearts burst out
Like water from a dam,
Deep echoes, full-throated,
Hit with a wham!

A Separate Peace

A look of amazement fell over him. It scared me, but I knew what I said was important and right, and my voice found that full tone voices have when they are expressing something long-felt and long-understood and released at last. (p. 182)

Show someone pouring out a long-held secret.

(3)

When on and on rattling
A little pause says "Oop!
I'd rather I wasn't tattling."
I'll just close the coop!

The Sea Wolf

"And you, too, seem a part of it. You are—" I was on the verge of saying, "my woman, my mate," but glibly changed it to—"standing the hardship well."

But her ear had caught the flaw. She recognized a flight that midmost broke. She gave me a quick look. (p. 202)

> Describe someone hesitating in mid-sentence and changing course.

(4)

When on the spot you're put
And it truly fazes you,
You feel a beaut, completely mute,
And then your voice betrays you.

Brave New World

A veneer of jaunty self-confidence thinly concealed his nervousness. The voice in which he said, "Good-morning, Director," was absurdly too loud; that in which, correcting his mistake, he said, "You asked me to come and speak to you here," ridiculously soft, a squeak. (p. 99)

> Record a conversation between a parent and a high schooler caught sneaking into the house after midnight.

(5)

Propaganda orator,
Conjuring enemy and traitor,
Elicits hatred and jeers,
Hoots, hollers, and fears.

Nineteen Eighty-four

A little Rumpelstiltskin figure, contorted with hatred, he gripped the neck of the microphone with one hand while the other, enormous at the end of a bony arm, clawed the air menacingly above his head...At every few minutes the fury of the crowd boiled over and the voice of the speaker was drowned by a wild beastlike roaring that rose uncontrollably from thousands of throats. (p. 149)

Describe how someone excites a crowd at a pep rally.

(6)

Accusations are serious shows,
As any commander knows.
He watches word and gesture
To discover friends and foes.

Billy Budd

"Shut the door there, sentry," said the commander. "Stand without and let nobody come in.—Now, Master-at-arms, tell this man to his face what you told of him to me;" and stood prepared to scrutinize the mutually confronting visages. (p. 65)

Tell how someone helps settle an argument.

(7)

Bravest knight, injured on bed,
Knows an important battle's ahead.
The clash of armies, the wheres and whys,
There it all is, seen through her eyes.

Ivanhoe

"Could I but reach yonder window!"
"Thou will but injure thyself by the attempt, noble knight," replied his attendant. Observing his extreme solicitude, she firmly added, "I myself will stand at the lattice, and describe to you as I can what passes without."
"God of Jacob! it is the meeting of two fierce tides - the conflict of two oceans moved by adverse winds!" (pp. 296 & 300)

Describe someone speaking on a phone, telling what's happening.

(8)

Prejudiced accusation, proud reply.
Verbal Ping-Pong, a party game.

Pride and Prejudice

"...your defect is a propensity to hate everybody."
"And yours," he replied with a smile, "is willfully to misunderstand them." (p. 51)

Describe a word duel between a girl and guy.

(9)

Squealer, wheeler-dealer, attention grabber,
Moves around, in tune, hypnotic gabber.

Animal Farm

All the other male pigs on the farm were porkers. The best known among them was a small fat pig named Squealer, with very round cheeks, twinkling eyes, nimble movements, and a shrill voice. He was a brilliant talker, and when he was arguing some difficult point he had a way of skipping from side to side and whisking his tail which was somehow very persuasive. The others said of Squealer that he could turn black into white. (p. 26)

> Describe how a popular student speaks and holds attention.

(10)

Gestures lend clout when off you spout.
They penetrate, captivate, pester, and flout.

Cry, the Beloved Country

—It is not my work to get lawyers, he says. It is my work to reform, to help, to uplift.
    With his hand he makes an angry gesture of uplifting, and then draws back his head into the car and makes as if to start. (p. 102)

> Describe gestures that support talk in a situation.

STUDY HINTS

Do your own work. Remember, you have personal ideas to put down and so does everyone else. Above all, do not borrow from a quoted passage.

Before you start, think through these words:

Nouns	Verbs	Adjectives	Adverbs
attention	bargain	annoying	cheerfully
conversation	flow	harsh	coyly
gesture	frown	hypnotic	frankly
giggle	hesitate	one-sided	gleefully
observer	interrupt	soothing	grimly
pause	lash	spell-binding	jokingly
smile	titter	trembling	mournfully

While working, turn to dictionaries for exact meanings and search in a synonym dictionary (thesaurus) for better words.

Before reading your finished product aloud, rehearse it until it sounds good. Read the way you talk only a bit slower and louder, remembering to pause between groups of ideas so everyone will "get it."

Begin most sentences low and smoothly raise the pitch to hit each word expressing a new idea. Practice reading this while moving your lips: "He carried the conversation along this way until we couldn't help laughing."

"Good readers make good writers."

CHAPTER 3. SIGN LANGUAGE

Facial and body gestures employ.
Be fearless and enjoy!
Accept a couple of chores and write 30-70 words each.
Check out the study hints for this chapter (page eighteen).

(1)

Sadness and sympathy, friend to friend,
A touch on the arm, "the weeping will end."

Cry, the Beloved Country

—Have courage, my brother.
He glanced at his friend, but Kumalo's eyes were on the ground.
Although Msimangu could not see his face, he could see the drop that fell on
the ground, and he tightened his grip on the arm. (p 64)

Describe helping hands when someone slips and falls.

(2)

His brother he needles - how he has scored!
He grabs his crop - it'll do for a sword!

Silas Marner

"Hold your tongue about Miss Nancy, you fool," said Godfrey, turn-
ing red, "else I'll throttle you."
"What for?" said Dunsey, still in an artificial tone, but taking a
whip from the table and beating the butt-end of it on his palm. (p. 31)

Describe someone grabbing an object to drive home a point.

(3)

What a weird wrinkle!
It's a message all right.
What does it bode?
Who has the code?

Heart of Darkness

He made no answer, but I saw a smile, a smile of indefinable meaning, appear on his colourless lips that a moment after twitched convulsively. (p. 145)

Describe a mysterious expression that comes over someone's face.

(4)

Oh, Billy, what have you done?
Killed a man without a gun!
In front of your commander too!
Billy, who will look out for you?

Billy Budd

Slowly he uncovered his face; forthwith the effect was as if the moon, emerging from eclipse, should reappear with quite another aspect than that which had gone into hiding. The father in him, manifested towards Billy thus far in the scene, was replaced by the military disciplinarian. (p. 67)

Describe a face changing after it is briefly covered.

(5)

The head can say "all right."
The head can say "no way!"
But does a geezer's nod mean something?
Or can it quite possibly mean nothing?

The Catcher in the Rye

He started going into this nodding routine...You never knew if he was nodding a lot because he was thinking and all, or just because he was a nice old guy that didn't know his ass from his elbow. (p. 12)

> Describe a handshake or hands on hips with unclear meaning.

(6)

Here we strain in the prison camp.
Slated to die and never decamp.
The faithful are fasting, including the pastor.
But I will live longer, defying disaster.

Night

As I swallowed my bowl of soup, I saw in the gesture an act of rebellion and protest against Him. (p. 66)

> Describe a small action of defiance against a person or system.

(7)

Describe how it happened?
Describe how it happened?
Here's the gimmick. Let me mimic.

A Tale of Two Cities

"He is bound as before, and in his mouth there is a gag - tied so, with a tight string, making him look almost as if you laughed." He suggested it by creasing his face with his two thumbs, from the corners of his mouth to his ears. (p. 215)

Describe a child mimicking a parent or a student mimicking a teacher.

(8)

"Watch out, Montag," the tube announces,
"The Mechanical Hound <u>always</u> pounces."
A meaningful look by trusted friend
Tells how the chase is certain to end.

Fahrenheit 451

Faber trembled the least bit and looked about at his house, at the walls, the door, the doorknob, and the chair where Montag now sat. Montag saw the look. (p. 145)

Describe a situation and a "telling" glance.

(9)

As Detective Lestrade delivers the news.
Reactions depend on various views.
The case once more is up in the air,
And Watson mindfully watches the pair.

Sherlock Holmes

The intelligence with which Lestrade greeted us was so momentous and so unexpected that we were all three fairly dumfounded. Gregson sprang out of his chair and upset the remainder of his whiskey and water. I stared in silence at Sherlock Holmes, whose lips were compressed and his brows drawn down over his eyes. (p. 46)

Describe reactions to a friend's announcement.

(10)

Kino and wife with child dead
Walk side by side and stride ahead.
I raise my hand to greet my friends.
But they look odd; my hand suspends.

The Pearl

Juan Tomas raised his hand in greeting and did not say the greeting and left his hand in the air for a moment uncertainly. (p. 116)

Describe raising a hand in class and hesitating.

STUDY HINTS

Do your own work. Remember, you have personal ideas to put down and so does everyone else. Above all, do not borrow from a quoted passage.

Before you start, think through these words:

Nouns	Verbs	Adjectives	Adverbs
blush	emphasize	cringing	bashfully
shake	gesture	flirting	mockingly
signal	nod	insulting	openly
slump	nudge	inviting	quickly
smile	point	reaching	quietly
tear	swallow	waving	secretly
twitch	wave	winking	smoothly

While working, turn to dictionaries for exact meanings and search in a synonym dictionary (thesaurus) for better words.

Before reading your finished product aloud, rehearse it until it sounds good. Read the way you talk only a bit slower and louder, remembering to pause between groups of ideas so everyone will "get it."

Begin most sentences low and smoothly raise the pitch to hit each word expressing a new idea. Practice reading this while moving your lips: "He spreads his <u>arms wide</u>, <u>raises</u> his <u>eyebrows</u>, and <u>lowers</u> the corners of his <u>mouth</u>."

"Good readers make good writers."

CHAPTER 4. ACTION ANGLES

For action write with conviction.
Be can-do in all your fiction,

Accept a couple of challenges and write 30-70 words each. Check out the study hints for this chapter (page twenty-four).

(1)
Accidental, fateful, coincidental,
And eerie, that's the theory.

One Flew Over the Cuckoo's Nest

I come out of the dorm into the hall just as McMurphy comes out of the latrine. (p. 84)

Describe a chance meeting, embarrassing or humorous.

(2)
Sailing from rival at bracing pace,
Taut, thrilling, close, windy chase.

The Sea Wolf

She was not running straight for us, but ahead of us. Our courses were converging like the sides of an angle, the vertex of which was at the edge of the fog-bank. (p. 164)

Describe catching up by a short cut.

(3)

Like raft floating on ocean,
A never-moving motion.
Frozen in space, locked in time,
Hanging like a rhyme.

Light in August

Though the mules plod in a steady and unflagging hypnosis, the vehicle does not seem to progress. It seems to hang suspended in the middle distance forever and forever, so infinitesimal is its progress, like a shabby bead upon the mild red string of road. (p. 7)

Describe the progress of a turtle crossing a road.

(4)

In car, bus, or train,
I gaze through rain,
Object stays to hold sight,
Scenes dash back in flight.

Orient Express

The village was so far from the line that it remained still, to be stared at, while the trees and cottages on the near bank, the tethered boats, fled backwards. (p. 47)

Describe a tall building, tower, or bridge with foreground in motion.

(5)

Huck and Jim serenely float
Upon the glorious river.
A demon steamer at their throat
Sends a panicky shiver.

The Adventures of Huckleberry Finn

She was a big one, and she was coming in a hurry, too, looking like a black cloud with rows of glow-worms around it; but all of a sudden she bulged out, big and scary, with a long row of wide-open furnace doors shining like red-hot teeth, and her monstrous bows and guards hanging right over us. (p. 85)

Describe a near miss when a huge vehicle bears down on a pedestrian by night.

(6)

What to the eye is verified?
A disappearance strange.
What to the mind is clarified?
An ordinary change.

Light in August

"He's at a dance...At a dance, you hear? He's not dancing, though." He laughed back, into the lamp; he turned his head and his laughing, running on up the stairs, vanishing as he ran, vanishing upward from the head down as if he were running headfirst and laughing into something that was obliterating him like a picture in chalk being erased from a blackboard. (p. 181)

Describe shoppers descending an escalator.

(7)

We ride the rails in light:
Headlong rush, wavering view,
Channel-switching, movie speed,
Snippets of sight, squeezed tight.

Orient Express

The world shifted and changed and passed them by. Trees and buildings rose and fell against a pale-blue clouded sky, beech changed to elm, and elm to fir, and fir to stone; a world, like lead upon a hot fire, bubbled into varying shapes now like a flame, now like a leaf of clover. (p. 58)

Describe a parade in fast-forward mode.

(8)

Not summer, spring, or fall
But winter when snow erases all.

Orient Express

The snow fell faster; the telegraph-poles along the line seemed glimpses of dark space in the gaps of a white wall. (p. 188)

Describe reflectors marking the roadway as seen in the high beam of a moving vehicle.

(9)

Alone with weaving devotion,
Coordinated, non-stop motion,
A spider or a weaver spinnin'
To finish Mrs. Osgood's linen.

Silas Marner

He seemed to weave, like the spider, from pure impulse, without reflection.
(p. 17)

Describe repeating movements of a work project.

(10)

Three on the run,
Taking a dare.
Three on a run,
Doing their share.

To Kill a Mockingbird

Jem threw open the gate and sped to the side of the house, slapped it with his palm and ran back past us, not waiting to see if his foray was successful. Dill and I followed on his heels. Safely on our porch, panting and out of breath, we looked back.
The old house was the same, droopy and sick, but as we stared down the street we thought we saw an inside shutter move. Flick. A tiny, almost invisible movement, and the house was still. (p. 21)

Describe a wild relay race.

STUDY HINTS

Do your own work. Remember, you have personal ideas to put down and so does everyone else. Above all, do not borrow from a quoted passage.

Before you start, think through these words:

Nouns	Verbs	Adjectives	Adverbs
approach	brake	clumsy	abruptly
collision	crowd	graceful	hesitantly
curve	gain	rowdy	jerkily
engine	muscle	slowing	speedily
force	pass	slow-moving	steadily
road	reach	suspicious	temporarily
turn	teeter	winged	waveringly

While working, turn to dictionaries for exact meanings and search in a synonym dictionary (thesaurus) for better words.

Before reading your finished product aloud, rehearse it until it sounds good. Read the way you talk only a bit slower and louder, remembering to pause between groups of ideas so everyone will "get it."

Begin most sentences low and smoothly raise the pitch to hit each word expressing a new idea. Practice reading this while moving your lips: "The car <u>leaves</u> the <u>coastal</u> city and motors to an overlooking <u>rise</u>."

"Good readers make good writers."

CHAPTER 5. WALK HINTS

You've "mastered" action, face, and talk;
It's time you learned to walk!

Choose a couple of activities and write 30-70 words each.
Check out the study hints for this chapter (page thirty).

(1)
Athlete leads smart set.
Walk graceful, fluid, no sweat.

A Separate Peace

Phineas just walked serenely on, or rather flowed on, rolling forward in his white sneakers with such unthinking unity of movement that "walk" didn't describe it. (p. 10)

Describe a non-athletic walk.

(2)
Commander of troops deals with foes.
Not like tramp, he strides a champ.

The Spy

Frances felt, as she walked by the side of this extraordinary man, that she was supported by one of no common stamp. The firmness of his step, and the composure of his manner, seemed to indicate a mind settled and resolved. (p. 296)

Describe the walk of a tramp.

(3)

When guys walk, girls watch.
When girls walk, guys watch.

My Antonia

But sometimes a young fellow would look up from his ledger, or out through the grating of his father's bank, and let his eyes follow Lena Lingard, as she passed the window with her slow, undulating walk, or Tiny Soderball, tripping by in her short skirt and striped stockings. (p. 160)

Describe two masculine walks that girls notice.

(4)

Walk in planes,
Lurch and lob.
Walk in trains,
Jiggle and bob.

Orient Express

The bony hand which held the pipe beat helplessly against his knee...A woman passed along the corridor, and for a moment all Mr. Savory's attention was visibly caught up to sail in her wake, bobbing, bobbing, bobbing, like his hand. (p. 73)

Describe someone walking the aisle of an airplane.

(5)

Man in forest
Sees birdgirl poorest,
Walking without fear
When snake is near.

Green Mansions

Seeing her thus, all those emotions of fear and abhorrence invariably excited in us by the sight of an active venomous serpent in our path vanished instantly from my mind: I could now only feel astonishment and admiration at the brilliant being as she advanced with swift, easy, undulating motion towards...the serpent... (p. 63)

Compare someone's walk to that of an animal.

(6)

Not on stroll,
Thoughts like coal,
Legs hardly work,
Move with jerk.

The Pearl

Kino and Juana walked through the city as though it were not there. Their eyes glanced neither right nor left nor up nor down, but stared only straight ahead. Their legs moved a little jerkily, like well-made wooden dolls, and they carried pillars of black fear about them. (p. 116)

Describe a dazed child walking from a wrecked car.

(7)

McMurphy, fit as fiddle,
Enters mental hospital.
The nurse orders force.
Handlers obey of course;
But they're Chicken Little.

One Flew Over the Cuckoo's Nest

This thought got them both at once and they froze, the big one and his tiny image, in exactly the same position, left foot forward, right hand out, half-way between Pete and the Big Nurse. (p. 52)

Describe a walker with a change of mind.

(8)

In the day our eyes spot a mouse;
At night we hear a snore.
We see and hear even more
At night sneaking up on a house.

Light in August

In the grass about his feet the crickets, which had ceased as he moved, keeping a little island of silence about him like thin yellow shadow of their small voices, began again, ceasing again when he moved with that tiny and alert suddenness...He walked without sound, moving in his tiny island of abruptly ceased insects. (p. 200)

Describe sounds on a night walk in a city.

(9)

From vantage point high or low,
What's visible is head or toe.

The Good Earth

From his hut where Wang Lung lay hid he heard hour after hour the passing of feet, the feet of soldiers marching to battle. Lifting sometimes a very little the mat which stood between them and him, he put one eye to the crack and he saw these feet passing, passing, leather shoes and cloth-covered legs, marching one after the other, pair by pair, score upon score, thousands upon thousands. (p. 94)

Describe the footgear of passersby in a mall.

(10)

Medieval marching is stately and right,
Marking a grieving lament.
A slow, curvy, drawn-out event
Like a long, long tail of a kite.

Ivanhoe

The priests of a neighbouring convent, in expectation of the ample donation, or soul-scat, which Cedric had propined, attended upon the cart in which the body of Athelstane was laid, and sang hymns as it was sadly and slowly borne on the shoulders of his vassals to his castle of Coningsburgh, to be there deposited in the grave of Hengist, from whom the deceased derived his long descent. (p. 337)

Describe walkers in a wedding or graduation ceremony.

STUDY HINTS

Do your own work. Remember, you have personal ideas
to put down and so does everyone else. Above all, do not
borrow from a quoted passage.
Before you start, think through these words:

Nouns	Verbs	Adjectives	Adverbs
bounce	continue	bent	aimlessly
glide	slip	dragging	casually
limp	sneak	erect	doubtfully
path	stride	marching	flowingly
rhythm	stroll	pacing	nervously
skip	tiptoe	shuffling	softly
step	wander	wobbling	unsteadily

While working, turn to dictionaries for exact meanings
and search in a synonym dictionary (thesaurus) for better
words.

Before reading your finished product aloud, rehearse it
until it sounds good. Read the way you talk only a bit slower
and louder, remembering to pause between groups of ideas so
everyone will "get it."

Begin most sentences low and smoothly raise the pitch to
hit each word expressing a new idea. Practice reading this
while moving your lips: "A fast city stride contrasts with a
leisurely country stroll."

"Good readers make good writers."

CHAPTER 6. OUTDOOR SHOTS

Walk out the door with a rush.
Get "cracking," bring your brush!

Choose a couple of exercises and write 30-70 words each.
Check out the study hints for this chapter (page thirty-six).

(1)

Let light play upon a scene.
A picture happens neat and clean.

Lord of the Flies

Here and there, little breezes crept over the polished waters beneath the haze of heat. When these breezes reached the platform the palm fronds would whisper, so that spots of blurred sunlight slid over their bodies or moved like bright, winged things in the shade. (p. 14)

Describe light on water at shore or beach.

(2)

From the window the camera shops,
Background rises, foreground hops.

The Great Gatsby

Over the great bridge, with the sunlight through the girders making a constant flicker upon the moving cars, with the city rising up across the river in white heaps and sugar lumps all built with a wish out of non-olfactory money. (p. 69)

Describe an approach to a city from an airplane.

(3)

Scenery to knock off sox,
Glare of the sun blocks.

For Whom the Bell Tolls

*The sun was in Robert Jordan's eyes and the bridge showed only in outline.
Then the sun lessened and was gone and looking up through the trees at the
brown, rounded height that it had gone behind, he saw, now, that he no longer
looked into the glare, that the mountain slope was a delicate new green and
that there were patches of old snow under the crest. (p. 35)*

Describe a glare blocking sight until viewer shifts position
or shades eyes.

(4)

Eyes take a skyward shift,
Spot a bird on the run.
A heron forceful, silvery, swift,
Prettied by moisture and sun.

The Return of the Native

*While she looked a heron arose on that side of the sky and flew on with his
face towards the sun. He had come dripping wet from some pool in the val-
leys, and as he flew the edges and lining of his wings, his thighs, and his
breast were so caught by the bright sunbeams that he appeared as if formed
of burnished silver. (p. 343)*

Picture a swimming fish, person, or animal caught in the
sun's rays.

(5)

Lack of motion for a spell,
Of radiance and quietness tell.
Charming three-dimensional power
Out on lawn in silent hour.

A Separate Peace

From behind us the last long rays of light played across the campus, accenting every slight undulation of the land, emphasizing the separateness of each bush. (p. 52)

Describe the hush of nature at a quiet time.

(6)

Back to the city, if you please.
In the evening when we take our ease.
To watch the sky in vibrant movement
And relish the tones of graphic pigment.

The Jungle

The line of buildings stood clear-cut and black against the sky; here and there out of the mass rose the great chimneys, with the rivers of smoke streaming away to the end of the world. It was a study in colors now, this smoke; in the sunset light it was black and brown and gray and purple. All the sordid suggestions of the place were gone - in the twilight it was a vision of power. (p. 34)

Describe the drama of the sky over a city in a daytime thunderstorm.

(7)

"Rain forest at evening"
Wins the ballot,
Shadows and light
From nature's palette.

Green Mansions

The sun was sinking behind the forest, its broad red disc still showing through the topmost leaves, and the higher part of the foliage was of a luminous green, like green flame, throwing off flakes of quivering, fiery light, but lower down the trees were in profound shadow. (p. 44)

Look up at the branches of a tree from underneath and describe what you see.

(8)

A lure of loveliness comes in the morning,
Before sun turns wicked without warning.

Their Eyes Were Watching God

Janie walked to the door with the pan in her hand still stirring the cornmeal dough and looked towards the barn. The sun from ambush was threatening the world with red daggers, but the shadows were gray and solid-looking around the barn. (p. 30)

Describe a photo opportunity in early morning light.

(9)

Fill your lungs with cool night air
And gather at the fire.
That was done in England fair
With permission of the squire.

The Return of the Native

The cheerful blaze streaked the inner surface of the human circle - now in-creased by other stragglers, male and female - with its own gold livery, and even overlaid the dark turf around with a lively luminousness, which soft-ened off into obscurity where the barrow rounded downwards out of sight. (p. 16)

Describe a campfire scene.

(10)

Silvery deck and ocean are a magic potion.

Billy Budd

There was a moderate sea at the time; and the moon, newly risen and near to being at its full, silvered the white spar-deck wherever not blotted by the clear-cut shadows horizontally thrown of fixtures and moving men. (p. 82)

Describe land in moonlight.

STUDY HINTS

Do your own work. Remember, you have personal ideas to put down and so does everyone else. Above all, do not borrow from a quoted passage.

Before you start, think through these words:

Nouns	Verbs	Adjectives	Adverbs
background	cross	breezy	charmingly
camera	gaze	dramatic	colorfully
field	glow	foggy	distantly
foreground	place	hazy	lonely
hill	reflect	shadowy	near
horizon	shine	tangled	skyward
wilderness	shower	wild	softly

While working, turn to dictionaries for exact meanings and search in a synonym dictionary (thesaurus) for better words.

Before reading your finished product aloud, rehearse it until it sounds good. Read the way you talk only a bit slower and louder, remembering to pause between groups of ideas so everyone will "get it."

Begin most sentences low and smoothly raise the pitch to hit each word expressing a new idea. Practice reading this while moving your lips: "There are <u>glorious</u> sunrises and <u>sunsets</u>, <u>buds</u> pearled with <u>dew</u>, and <u>leaves</u> that look like <u>butterflies</u>."

"Good readers make good writers."

CHAPTER 7. PATTERNS AND DESIGNS

Words fall into place, ideas unfold,
Drawing objects manifold.

Choose a couple of suggestions and write 30-70 words each.
Check out the study hints for this chapter (page forty-two).

(1)

In counties near and countries far
Leaves and trees and branches are.

Green Mansions

Just before me, where I sat, grew a low, widespreading plant, covered with broad, round, polished leaves; and the roundness, stiffness, and perfectly horizontal position of the upper leaves made them look like a collection of small platforms or round tabletops placed nearly on a level. (p. 51)

Describe an interesting flower, bush, or branch.

(2)

Birds and animals colorful are
In counties near and countries far.

Green Mansions

Viewing it closely, I found that it was a coral snake, famed as much for its beauty and singularity as for its deadly character...It was about three feet long, and very slim; its ground color a brilliant vermilion, with broad jet-black rings at equal distances round its body, each black ring or band divided by a narrow yellow strip in the middle. (p. 62)

Describe a bird or animal by color and design.

(3)

An amphitheater surrounds the ground.
Shapes and splashes of color abound.

Ivanhoe

The lists now presented a most splendid spectacle. The sloping galleries were crowded with all that was noble, great, wealthy, and beautiful in the northern and midland parts of England; and the contrast of the various dresses of these dignified spectators, rendered the view as gay as it was rich, while the interior and lower space, filled with the substantial burgesses and yeomen of merry England, formed, in their more plain attire, a dark fringe, or border, around this circle of brilliant embroidery, relieving, and, at the same time, setting off its splendor. (p. 81)

Describe fans in bleachers at a game.

(4)

Grass, breezes, flags, and waves -
All these the interior saves.

The Great Gatsby

We walked through a high hallway into a bright rosy-colored space, fragilely bound into the house by French windows at either end. The windows were ajar and gleaming white against the fresh grass outside that seemed to grow a little way into the house. A breeze blew through the room, blew curtains in at one end and out the other like pale flags, twisting them up toward the frosted wedding-cake of the ceiling, and then rippled over the wine-colored rug, making a shadow on it as wind does on the sea. (p. 8)

Describe a lobby, office, library, or any room that brings the outdoors in.

(5)

Barnacle-encrusted oysters
Are ripped apart by divers.
Long since they have fled,
Leaving behind an unmade bed.

The Pearl

Light filtered down through the water to the bed where the frilly pearl oysters lay fastened to the rubbly bottom, a bottom strewn with shells of broken, opened oysters. (p. 21)

Describe a trashed bedroom or littered roadside or vacant lot.

(6)

A group of colored dots in motion,
Moving to and from the ocean.

The Heart of Darkness

Flames glided in the river, small green flames, red flames, white flames, pursuing, overtaking, joining, crossing each other - then separating slowly or hastily. The traffic of the great city went on in the deepening night upon the sleepless river. (p. 70)

Describe air traffic over a city after dark.

(7)

Thousands of leaves on a birch tree,
Delicate pattern and form.
If you really want to count, feel free!
Choose a lovely day and warm.

The Return of the Native

Venn soon after went away, and in the evening Yeobright strolled as far as Fairway's cottage. It was a lovely May sunset, and the birch trees which grew on this margin of the vast Egdon wilderness had put on their new leaves, delicate as butterflies' wings, and diaphanous as amber. (p. 458)

Describe the bark and leaves of your favorite tree.

(8)

Oval leaves of a pear tree, each pointed at the end,
Haphazard breezes sway in moonlight ray.

The House of Seven Gables

Observe that silvery dance upon the upper branches of the pear tree, and now a little lower, and now on the whole mass of boughs, while, through their shifting intricacies, the moonbeams fall aslant into the room. (p. 242)

Describe light and shadows formed by a car's headlights.

(9)

Dogs and birds leave tracks,
So do snakes.
Shoes and tires leave tracks,
So do rakes.

Ethan Frome

She moved forward a step or two and then paused again above the dip of the Corbury road. Its icy slope, scored by innumerable runners, looked like a mirror scratched by travellers at an inn. (p. 45)

Describe a cluster of footprints or tire tracks or doodling on a telephone pad.

(10)

In a carload of death, little breath.
Gruesome to behold, a tangled fold.

Night

When at last a gray glimmer of light appeared on the horizon, it revealed a tangle of human shapes, heads sunk upon shoulders, crouched, piled one on top of the other, like a field of dust-covered tombstones in the first light of the dawn. (p. 93)

Picture a crowd on a subway, bus, or train, or in a waiting room.

STUDY HINTS

Do your own work. Remember, you have personal ideas to put down and so does everyone else. Above all, do not borrow from a quoted passage.

Before you start, think through these words:

Nouns	Verbs	Adjectives	Adverbs
border	circle	defined	amply
distance	copy	etched	closely
map	expose	ever changing	colorfully
network	hide	grouped	exactly
space	merge	scattered	regularly
spiral	repeat	separated	similarly
surface	vary	unplanned	straight

While working, turn to dictionaries for exact meanings and search in a synonym dictionary (thesaurus) for better words.

Before reading your finished product aloud, rehearse it until it sounds good. Read the way you talk only a bit slower and louder, remembering to pause between groups of ideas so everyone will "get it."

Begin most sentences low and smoothly raise the pitch to hit each word expressing a new idea. Practice reading this while moving your lips: "These patterns are uniform, like wallpaper designs."

"Good readers make good writers."

CHAPTER 8. SENSE SCENES

Crystal clear expression
Just around the corner.

Accept a couple of jobs and write 30-70 words each.
Check out the study hints for this chapter (page forty-eight).

(1)
Flower drenched in sun.
Garden sunlight fun.

The Return of the Native

"Ah, my!" said Eustacia, with a laugh which unclosed her lips so that the sun shone into her mouth as into a tulip and lent it a similar scarlet fire. (p. 104)

Describe faces lighted by flashlights in silly ways.

(2)
Wearing gear feels queer;
Weight pressing down all the way to town.

The Red Badge of Courage

His canteen banged rhythmically upon his thigh, and his haversack bobbed softly. His musket bounced a trifle from his shoulder at each stride and made his cap feel uncertain upon his head. (p. 40)

Describe wearing sports equipment or backpacking on a trail.

(3)

Winston and Julia hide in town,
Thought-police hunt them down.
Though they abuse her by his side,
He dares not turn his head aside.

Nineteen Eighty-four

Winston dared not turn his head even by a millimeter, but sometimes her livid, gasping face came within the angle of his vision. (p. 184)

Describe someone with a neck brace trying to watch a tennis match.

(4)

Sudden changes catch the eye,
Light cut off or movement sly.

Of Mice and Men

Both men glanced up, for the rectangle of sunshine in the doorway was cut off. A girl was standing there looking in. (p. 31)

Describe seeing something move, out of the corner of the eye.

(5)

Being out and coming to,
Eyes rest on the foreground.
Then they take in what's around,
Other objects are there too.

Night

The operation lasted an hour. They had not put me to sleep. I kept my eyes fixed upon my doctor. Then I felt myself go under...

When I came round, opening my eyes, I could see nothing at first but a great whiteness, my sheets; then I noticed the face of my doctor, bending over me... (p. 75)

Describe vision upon waking from sleep in the light of day.

(6)

Coral, still woozy, has fainted;
Her view of the world is tainted.
In her mind she's still standing,
Must rethink her crash-landing.

Orient Express

The girl came back to a confusing consciousness; she thought that it was she who was bending over a stranger with a long, shabby moustache...She put her hands down to his face. He's ill, she thought, and for a moment shut out the puzzling shadows which fell the wrong way, the globe of light shining from the ground. (p. 32)

Describe vision during a fall or a spin.

(7)

Sounds to ear out of range, strange.
Sounds to ear in range, arrange.

The Return of the Native

With nearer approach these fragmentary sounds became pieced together, and were found to be the salient points of the tune called "Nancy's Fancy." (p. 154)

Describe the approach of a marching band.

(8)

Partial quiet,
Clatter loud,
Echo loud,
Absolute quiet.

Heart of Darkness

I tried a jig. We capered on the iron deck. A frightful clatter came out of that hulk, and the virgin forest on the other bank of the creek sent it back in a thundering roll upon the sleeping station...We stopped, and the silence driven away by the stamping of our feet flowed back again from the recesses of the land. (p.98)

Describe an indoor echo.

(9)

An old man is straining,
Fighting the catch of his life.
His mind starts explaining
A taste like the cut of a knife.

The Old Man and the Sea

The old man could hardly breathe now and he felt a strange taste in his mouth. It was coppery and sweet and he was afraid of it for a moment. But there was not much of it. (p. 119)

> Describe a stressful circumstance and the taste of blood, sweat, or tears.

(10)

Soldier in wartime finds safe bay,
Breathes full-flavored hay
That triggers an image
Far from the scrimmage.

A Farewell to Arms

The hay smelled good and lying in a barn in the hay took away all the years in between. We had lain in hay and talked and shot sparrows with an air-rifle when they perched in the triangle cut high up in the wall of the barn. (p. 216)

> Describe taste or odor bringing back memories.

STUDY HINTS

Do your own work. Remember, you have personal ideas to put down and so does everyone else. Above all, do not borrow from a quoted passage.

Before you start, think through these words:

Nouns	Verbs	Adjectives	Adverbs
confusion	approach	alert	dimly
focus	echo	dancing	distinctly
glimmer	feel	flavored	instantly
noise	glance	golden	obviously
sunbeam	listen	hushed	shrilly
tang	pierce	leaving	unawares
thought	remember	stinking	visibly

While working, turn to dictionaries for exact meanings and search in a synonym dictionary (thesaurus) for better words.

Before reading your finished product aloud, rehearse it until it sounds good. Read the way you talk only a bit slower and louder, remembering to pause between groups of ideas so everyone will "get it."

Begin most sentences low and smoothly raise the pitch to hit each word expressing a new idea. Practice reading this while moving your lips: "Sounds are pleasant or painful, too low or too loud."

"Good readers make good writers."

CHAPTER 9. SENSE VARIETY

Be patient and don't tire,
Your writing will catch fire!

Choose a couple of exercises and write 30-70 words each.
Check out the study hints for this chapter (page fifty-four).

(1)

Back in the sack like a fool,
Warm and cozy, warm and cool.

Light in August

The shades were drawn and she lay still in the more than halfdark, on her back. Her eyes were closed and her face was empty and smooth. After a while she began to open her legs and close them slowly, feeling the sheets flow cool and smooth over them and then flow warm and smooth again. (p. 113)

Describe a hot shower that turns icy.

(2)

Raising an oar handle to shock a shark,
Today at least, fishing's no lark!

The Old Man and the Sea

...he raised the club high and brought it down heavy and slamming onto the top of the shark's broad head. He felt the rubbery solidity as the club came down. But he felt the rigidity of bone too... (p. 113)

Describe the feel of a worm and a hook, a necklace and skin, or sand in a slipper.

(3)

Who's that singing in a tree
Mocking my society,
Horning, scorning, mourning?
What impropriety!

To Kill a Mockingbird

High above us in the darkness a solitary mocker poured out his repertoire in blissful unawareness of whose tree he sat in, plunging from the shrill kee, kee of the sunflower bird to the irascible qua-ack of the bluejay, to the sad lament of Poor Will, Poor Will. (p. 268)

Describe switching music stations on a radio.

(4)

Rev the engine, shift the gear,
Press the pedal, cock the ear.
The pitch rises higher than ever.
Man, is flying clever!

Brave New World

He started the engines and threw the helicopter screws into gear. The machine shot vertically into the air. Henry accelerated; the humming of the propeller shrilled from hornet to wasp, from wasp to mosquito...

He took his foot off the accelerator. The humming of the screws overhead dropped an octave and a half, back through wasp and hornet to bumble bee, to cockchafer, to stag-beetle. (pp. 40 & 41)

Describe change in pitch for a car, musical instrument, or voice.

(5)

A nose jailed in cave
Some fresh air might crave.

For Whom the Bell Tolls

There was no wind, and, outside of the warm air of the cave...away now from the copper-penny, red wine and garlic, horse sweat and man sweat dried in the clothing (acrid and gray the man sweat, sweet and sickly the dried brushed-off lather of horse sweat), of the men at the table, Robert Jordan breathed deeply of the clear night air of the mountains that smelled of the pines and of the dew on the grass in the meadow by the stream. (p. 59)

Describe contrary scents in a restaurant or home.

(6)

Stale odors repeat, repeat,
But check out this man Pete.
He luckily brings good news
To replace yucky PU's!

One Flew Over the Cuckoo's Nest

Sweeping the dorm soon's it's empty, I'm after dust mice under his bed when I get a smell of something that makes me realize for the first time since I been in the hospital that this big dorm full of beds, sleeps forty grown men, has always been sticky with a thousand other smells - smells of germicide, zinc ointment, and foot powder, smell of piss and sour old-man manure, of Pablum and eyewash, of musty shorts and socks musty even when they're fresh back from the laundry, the stiff odor of starch in the linen, the acid stench of morning mouths, the banana smell of machine oil, and sometimes the smell of singed hair - but never before now, before he came in, the man smell of dust and dirt from the open fields, and sweat, and work. (p. 91)

Describe distinct odors in a dressing room, locker room, or barn.

(7)

Jingle, jangle, tap, and clatter.
In a train these things matter.
Yet they numb the ear and fade away
Upon the train's getaway.

Orient Express

But in the rushing reverberating express, noise was so regular that it was the equivalent of silence, movement was so continuous that after a while the mind accepted it as stillness. (p. 23)

Describe a sound we tend to ignore: traffic, radios, machinery, etc.

(8)

A "deep, harsh note" lets out a yell,
Echoing to the beach from the mountain.
Ralph has sounded the conch shell,
Making voice soft as fountain.

Lord of the Flies

Ralph took the shell away from his lips. "Gosh!" His ordinary voice sounded like a whisper after the harsh note of the conch. (p. 16)

Describe the sound of a voice after a blaring noise: public address system, theft alarm, "yelper," etc.

(9)

Choir of children, practicing hymns,
Tunes at back of church.
Joe Christmas, behaving crudely,
Breaks the harmony rudely.

Light in August

The door had not been locked or even shut yet the man had apparently grasped it by the knob and hurled it back into the wall so that the sound crashed into the blended voices like a pistol shot. (p. 281)

Describe a loud noise scattering a flock of birds.

(10)

Knife slash or bullet wound
Invades nerves and gore.
Warming sun or creeping fly,
Attend to them? What for?

For Whom the Bell Tolls

His head was in the shadow but the sun shone on his plugged and bandaged wound and on his hands that were cupped over it...A fly crawled on his hands but the small tickling did not come through the pain. (p. 442)

Describe a nuisance feeling in the midst of serious pain.

STUDY HINTS

Do your own work. Remember, you have personal ideas
to put down and so does everyone else. Above all, do not
borrow from a quoted passage.

Before you start, think through these words:

Nouns	Verbs	Adjectives	Adverbs
banquet	caress	aware	constantly
collision	change	covered	harshly
hunger	hug	delightful	internally
odor	recognize	flashy	keenly
shake	tickle	painful	richly
silence	tune in	sharp	slightly
whisper	vibrate	velvety	wholly

While working, turn to dictionaries for exact meanings
and search in a synonym dictionary (thesaurus) for better
words.

Before reading your finished product aloud, rehearse it
until it sounds good. Read the way you talk only a bit slower
and louder, remembering to pause between groups of ideas so
everyone will "get it."

Begin most sentences low and smoothly raise the pitch to
hit each word expressing a new idea. Practice reading this
while moving your lips: "What etches itself in memory?
Freshly ground coffee, the whiff of meats and pies cooking,
and smoke from fires."

"Good readers make good writers."

CHAPTER 10. THE SENSES MIXED

All the possibilities to sup.
Shouldn't it fire you up?
Accept a couple of tasks and write 30-70 words each.
Check out the study hints for this chapter (page sixty).

(1)
What do we never forget?
Events we never met!

Black Boy

There was the fear and awe I felt when Grandpa took me to a sawmill to watch the giant whirring steel blades whine and scream as they bit into wet green logs. (p. 54)

Mixing senses, describe a first-time childhood experience: amusement park, circus, live theater, sports event, etc.

(2)
Here's a childhood memory too;
Think of it as new.
All five senses are on call
For the best description of all.

The Keys of the Kingdom

Thereafter the day was heady with the sound of the stream, the scent of meadowsweet - his father showing him the likely eddies, - the crimson-speckled trout wriggling on bleached shingle, - his father bent over a twig fire, - the crisp sweet goodness of the frizzled fish... (p. 15)

Describe with all the senses an experience from childhood.

(3)

The odor is personal, no matter the weather:
Schoolrooms, shops, houses, whatever.

The Catcher in the Rye

It was dark as hell in the foyer, naturally, and naturally I couldn't turn on any lights. I had to be careful not to bump into anything and make a racket. I certainly knew I was home, though. Our foyer has a funny smell that doesn't smell like anyplace else. I don't know what the hell it is. It isn't cauliflower and it isn't perfume - I don't know what the hell it is - but you always know you're home. (p. 205)

Discuss sense oddities of a special place.

(4)

Feels to the foot,
Colors that stay,
Smells full-blown,
Sounds well known,
Folded into memory
Day after day.

Orient Express

She had said the slums were the same, and he could feel under his feet the steep steps down into the narrow gorges; he bent under the bright rags stretched across the way, put his handkerchief across his mouth to shut out the smell of dogs, of children, of bad meat and human ordure...Five years was a long time, he might already be forgotten. (p. 51)

Describe a party lasting in memory.

(5)

Journey far, travel and realize,
Venture beyond the homeland you know.
New sensations for ears and eyes,
New for nose, tongue, and toe.

The Grapes of Wrath

And the hot breath of the valley came up to them, with hot green smells on it, and with resinous sage and tarweed smells. The crickets crackled along the road. A rattlesnake crawled across the road and Tom hit it and broke it and left it squirming. (p. 296)

Mixing senses, describe a brand new scene.

(6)

Wagon and mules,
Hanging like fools,
Sound retort,
A weather report.

Light in August

The sharp and brittle crack and clatter of its weathered and ungreased wood and metal is slow and terrific: a series of dry sluggish reports carrying for a half mile across the hot still pinewiney silence of the August afternoon. (p. 7)

Describe a locality through the senses of a hiker or biker.

(7)

Room secure, room at peace,
Senses calm, sure release.

Ethan Frome

Deep quiet sank on the room. The clock ticked above the dresser, a piece
of charred wood fell now and then in the stove, and the faint sharp scent of
the geraniums mingled with the odour of Ethan's smoke, which began to
throw a blue haze about the lamp and to hang its greyish cobwebs in the
shadowy corners of the room. (p. 90)

Mixing senses, describe a quiet place.

(8)

Hearing and seeing abound,
Notice smells around.
Fragrances   fill   page;
Garden fumes set stage.

Jane Eyre

Sweet briar and southern wood, jasmine, pink, and rose, have long been
yielding their evening sacrifice of incense: this new scent is neither of shrub
nor flower; it is - I know it well - it is Mr. Rochester's cigar. I look round and
I listen. I see trees laden with ripening fruit. I hear a nightingale
warbling in a wood half a mile off; no moving form is visible, no coming step
audible; but that perfume increases: I must flee. (p. 279)

Describe a garden or yard as a feast for the senses.

(9)

Last hum of squadron run,
Touch delicate, finespun.

For Whom the Bell Tolls

There was not even the last almost unheard hum that comes like a finger faintly touching and leaving and touching again after the sound is gone almost part hearing. (p. 88)

Compare turning off a radio to a clap of the hand.

(10)

Tender kiss of woman's hair,
To what does it compare?
Sawdust for smell, moss for feel.
That's what the senses reveal.

Ethan Frome

She clung to him without answering, and he laid his lips on her hair, which was soft yet springy, like certain mosses on warm slopes, and had the faint woody fragrance of fresh sawdust in the sun. (p. 146)

Compare a kiss to a bite of a chocolate bar.

STUDY HINTS

Do your own work. Remember, you have personal ideas to put down and so does everyone else. Above all, do not borrow from a quoted passage.

Before you start, think through these words:

Nouns	Verbs	Adjectives	Adverbs
bitterness	applaud	brilliant	clearly
blend	echo	confusing	faintly
flavor	handle	fiery	fittingly
focus	listen	frosty	fragrantly
glint	pierce	shadowy	gently
memory	rebound	sore	noisily
variety	swell	stimulating	simply

While working, turn to dictionaries for exact meanings and search in a synonym dictionary (thesaurus) for better words.

Before reading your finished product aloud, rehearse it until it sounds good. Read the way you talk only a bit slower and louder, remembering to pause between groups of ideas so everyone will "get it."

Begin most sentences low and smoothly raise the pitch to hit each word expressing a new idea. Practice reading this while moving your lips: "He wakes on a rocking ship, hears rattling pans, and feels rough hands chafing his chest."

"Good readers make good writers."

CHAPTER 11. PRIVATE THOUGHTS

Maybe you were designed
To write what goes on in the mind!

Accept a couple of chores and write 30-70 words each.
Check out the study hints for this chapter (page sixty-six).

(1)

Dialogue overlaps in weird ways.
To sort it out might take days.

Jane Eyre

...suddenly I discovered that my ear was wholly intent on analysing the mingled sounds, and trying to discriminate amidst the confusion of accents those of Mr. Rochester; and when it caught them, which it soon did, it found a further task in framing the tones, rendered by distance inarticulate, into words. (p. 191)

Describe an attempt to spot someone in a crowd.

(2)

Gathering data, sizing up facts,
The inquiring mind can never relax.

Sherlock Holmes

"By a man's finger-nails, by his coat-sleeve, by his boots, by his trouser-knees, by the callosities of his forefinger and thumb, by his expression, by his shirt-cuffs - by each of these things a man's calling is plainly revealed." (p. 23)

Describe someone analyzing the handwriting of an unsigned letter.

(3)

Think everything through, Silas Marner.
Look out for yourself and garner, garner!

Silas Marner

Silas was thinking with double complacency of his supper: first, because it would be hot and savory; and secondly, because it would cost him nothing. (p. 50)

> Describe the self-satisfied thoughts of someone driving a car.

(4)

In the precincts of the mind
The mill grinds along.
Be it criminal or kind,
Under pressure it thinks its song.

Orient Express

I can't be caught, he thought incredulously...and waited with his back to the yard for a word or a bullet, while his brain began to move like the little well-oiled wheels of a watch, one thought fitting into another and setting a third in motion. (p. 94)

> Describe thinking under pressure at school, home, or work.

(5)

Here's Imlac using his bean,
Putting himself in another's shoes.
His logic is "super-keen"!
That way how can he lose?

The History of Rasselas

"Every man," said Imlac, "may, by examining his own mind, guess what passes in the minds of others: when you feel that your own gaiety is counterfeit, it may justly lead you to suspect that of your companions not to be sincere." (p. 77)

Analyze other people in light of your own habits or attitudes.

(6)

To cross the desert in the family truck,
A woman sits while Granma dies,
Not giving her proper goodbyes.
But that's just poor folks' luck.

The Grapes of Wrath

The family looked at Ma with a little terror at her strength.
Tom said, "Jesus Christ! You layin' there with her all night long!"
"The fambly hadda get acrost," Ma said miserably. (p. 294)

Describe a dialogue revealing a brave child's reasoning.

(7)

The adulteress stands in the ordained spot,
Analyzing her sullied life.
Her babe in arms will share her lot
And the man there who made her his wife.

The Scarlet Letter

While this passed, Hester Prynne had been standing on her pedestal, still with a fixed gaze towards the stranger; so fixed a gaze, that, at moments of intense absorption, all other objects in the visible world seemed to vanish, leaving only him and her. (p. 50)

Describe the thoughts of a student sent out for unacceptable behavior in class.

(8)

At the tail of a crowded day
An active mind has its say.
A "grab-bag" to recollect.

A Tale of Two Cities

Rustling about the room, his softly-slippered feet making no noise on the floor, he moved like a refined tiger...He moved from end to end of his voluptuous bedroom, looking again at the scraps of the day's journey that came unbidden into his mind... (p. 158)

Portray evening thoughts of a teen recalling the day.

(9)

Her secret voice is like a trumpet,
"Beware!" - like it or lump it.

Jane Eyre

...I thought, "No; impossible! my supposition cannot be correct." "Yet," suggested the secret voice which talks to us in our own hearts..."last night - remember his words; remember his look; remember his voice!"
I well remembered all: language, glance, and tone seemed at the moment vividly renewed. (p. 179)

Portray a struggle with an inner voice.

(10)

A dream mirrors reality
As true as noon light.
It uses a plot
As false as twilight.

The Pearl

But Kino's brain burned, even during his sleep, and he dreamed that Coyotito could read, that one of his own people could tell him the truth of things. And in his dream, Coyotito was reading from a book as large as a house, with letters as big as dogs, and the words galloped and played on the book. (p. 47)

Discuss a dream about being ten feet tall or ten inches small.

STUDY HINTS

Do your own work. Remember, you have personal ideas to put down and so does everyone else. Above all, do not borrow from a quoted passage.

Before you start, think through these words:

Nouns	Verbs	Adjectives	Adverbs
brain		cope with	absorbed
alertly			
conscience	fathom	awed	contentedly
craving	notice	conspicuous	dreamily
effort	sift	crystal-clear	drowsily
hunch	trust	hidden	idly
quest	understand	honorable	nobly
wish	wrestle	scared	prayerfully

While working, turn to dictionaries for exact meanings and search in a synonym dictionary (thesaurus) for better words.

Before reading your finished product aloud, rehearse it until it sounds good. Read the way you talk only a bit slower and louder, remembering to pause between groups of ideas so everyone will "get it."

Begin most sentences low and smoothly raise the pitch to hit each word expressing a new idea. Practice reading this while moving your lips: "Dust off your memories, draw on your talents, and sharpen your logic."

"Good readers make good writers."

CHAPTER 12. EMOTIONAL DISPLAYS

Take feelings off the shelf;
Be patient with yourself.

Accept a couple of challenges and write 30-70 words each.
Check out the study hints for this chapter (page seventy-two).

(1)

In a room a brother hush
Ducks an adrenaline rush.

To Kill a Mockingbird

...I entered the livingroom. Atticus had retreated behind his newspaper and Aunt Alexandra was worrying her embroidery. Punk, punk, punk, her needle broke the taut circle. She stopped, and pulled the cloth tighter: punk-punk-punk. She was furious. (p. 147)

Describe a furious coach with a "short fuse."

(2)

The bunkhouse boys avoid his room in the stable.
By visitors he's pleased; to hide it he's unable.

Of Mice and Men

Crooks said irritably, "You can come in if you want."
Candy seemed embarrassed. "I do' know. 'Course if ya want me to."
"Come on in. If ever'body's comin' in, you might just as well." It was diffi-cult for Crooks to conceal his pleasure with anger. (p. 74)

Describe a poker player unable to keep a straight face with a winning hand.

(3)

Drunken sounds of sailors surround.
There's no help, guard, or legal aid.
Another guy, wooing his girl, gains ground.
He's bummed, jealous, ticked off, afraid.

The Sea Wolf

And all the while I sat in a half-daze, the drunken riot of the steerage breaking through the bulkhead, the man I feared and the woman I loved talking on and on. (p. 172)

Describe watching someone at a party enjoy the one you came with.

(4)

Emotions show colors true:
Turn white, see red, feel blue.
His face is white; he's cornered like a swine;
His career and life on the line.

Billy Budd

Not at first did Billy take it in. When he did the rose-tan of his cheek looked struck as by white leprosy. He stood like one impaled and gagged. (p. 66)

Describe an innocent student accused of wrongdoing.

(5)

Priest volunteers,
Past interferes,
No friendly note,
Lump in throat.

Orient Express

Dr. Czinner drew the door to and sat down in the opposite seat. "You are a priest?" He tried to add "father," but the word stuck on his tongue; it meant too much, it meant a grey starved face, affection hardening into respect, sacrifice into suspicion of a son grown like an enemy. (p. 138)

Describe the triggering of a bitter memory.

(6)

Mother proud and bad,
Living aloof in open.
Father, hidden and sad,
Having trouble copin'.

The Scarlet Letter

Happy are you, Hester, that wear the scarlet letter openly upon your bosom! Mine burns in secret! Thou little knowest what a relief it is, after the torment of a seven years' cheat, to look into an eye that recognizes me for what I am! (p. 135)

Describe someone bothered by a guilty secret.

(7)

A verse moves Mrs. Phelps to tears.
Her face becomes rubbery.
Her voice, blubbery.
She hasn't cried in years.

Fahrenheit 451

Mrs. Phelps was crying.
The others in the middle of the dessert watched her crying grow very loud as her face squeezed itself out of shape. They sat, not touching her, bewildered with her display. She sobbed uncontrollably. Montag himself was stunned and shaken. (p. 109)

Describe someone "tearing up" over a film.

(8)

A boxcar crammed with prisoners,
Everyone on edge.
Someone begins to shriek and shout.
Everyone could freak out!

Night

Our terror was about to burst the sides of the train. Our nerves were at breaking point. Our flesh was creeping. It was as though madness were taking possession of us all. We could stand it no longer. Some of the young men forced her to sit down, tied her up, and put a gag in her mouth. (p. 23)

Tell how someone "cracks up," becoming hysterical.

(9)

He cries the echo of death
When his love loses breath.

The Jungle

*He clutched her hands, he shook her, he caught her in his arms and pressed
her to him; but she lay cold and still - she was gone - she was gone!*

*The word rang through him like the sound of a bell, echoing in the far depths
of him, making forgotten chords to vibrate, old shadowy fears to stir - fears
of the dark, fears of the void, fears of annihilation...He was like a little child,
in his fright and grief; he called and called, and got no answer, and his cries
of despair echoed through the house, making the women downstairs draw
nearer to each other in fear. (p. 189)*

> Describe a personal grief at the moment of death in a
> fictional setting.

(10)

Husband, friend, hero, lover,
To Janie that was Tea Cake.
The ground is now his cover.
Her mourning is not fake.

Their Eyes Were Watching God

*No expensive veils and robes for Janie this time. She went on in her overalls.
She was too busy feeling grief to dress like grief. (p. 180)*

> Describe someone's thoughts at a burial.

STUDY HINTS

Do your own work. Remember, you have personal ideas to put down and so does everyone else. Above all, do not borrow from a quoted passage.

Before you start, think through these words:

Nouns	Verbs	Adjectives	Adverbs
crosscurrent	control	choked-up	bitterly
guilt	cry	enraged	frightfully
instinct	faint	flushed	furiously
relief	incite	isolated	resentfully
struggle	stir	pale	shockingly
switch	thrill	petrified	violently
tension	worry	storm-tossed	wearily

While working, turn to dictionaries for exact meanings and search in a synonym dictionary (thesaurus) for better words.

Before reading your finished product aloud, rehearse it until it sounds good. Read the way you talk only a bit slower and louder, remembering to pause between groups of ideas so everyone will "get it."

Begin most sentences low and smoothly raise the pitch to hit each word expressing a new idea. Practice reading this while moving your lips: "Her face showed <u>surprise</u>, but when she had learned what <u>happened</u>, she calmed <u>down</u>."

"Good readers make good writers."

CHAPTER 13. IMAGINATION IMAGES

Nail high-flying prances;
Take chances!

Choose a couple of activities and write 30-70 words each. Check out the study hints for this chapter (page seventy-eight).

(1)

Remembering London is no strain
Roaring through Europe on a train.

Orient Express

Away from the rattling metal, the beating piston, she stepped in thought, wrapping a fur coat round her, up the stairs to her flat. (p. 125)

Describe someone traveling far away and remembering home.

(2)

Like father, like son; like mother, like daughter.

Orient Express

For that moment she was her mother; she had sloughed her own experiences as easily as a dress, the feigned gentility of the theatre, the careful speech. "Who do you think you are?" (p. 126)

Describe a son taking on the role of his dad for a moment.

(3)

Put war on hold,
Forget fate of bold.
Turn to a loved one's lair
Behind the fall of her hair.

A Farewell to Arms

...I would watch her while she kept very still and then take out the last two pins and it would all come down and she would drop her head and we would both be inside of it, and it was the feeling of inside a tent or behind a falls. (p.114)

Pretend driving a car with a date is a ride through outer space.

(4)

Best corn country in world,
Not New York, Texas, or Alaska.
Best corn country in world,
Plains of Kansas and Nebraska.

My Antonia

If all the great plain from the Missouri to the Rocky Mountains had been under glass, and the heat regulated by a thermometer, it could not have been better for the yellow tassels that were ripening and fertilizing the silk day by day. (p. 110)

Compare an entire ocean to a fish tank.

(5)

The game of leapfrog, blood is pulsing.
I may be top dog, but I'd rather be waltzing!

A Tale of Two Cities

Except on the crown which was raggedly bald, he had stiff, black hair, standing jaggedly all over it, and growing downhill almost to his broad, blunt nose. It was so...like the top of a strongly spiked wall...that the best players at leapfrog might have declined him, as the most dangerous man in the world to go over. (p. 17)

Describe what a head a hair reminds you of.

(6)

Shadow walking, what a sight!
Shadow walking, yah, right!

Heart of Darkness

The sun was low; and leaning forward side by side, they seemed to be tugging painfully uphill their two ridiculous shadows of unequal length, that trailed behind them slowly over the tall grass without bending a single blade. (p. 102)

Describe pictures imagined in summer cloud formations.

(7)

Raw recruit dreams a salute
By envious lads and battle grads.

The Red Badge of Courage

Swift pictures of himself, apart, yet in himself, came to him - a blue desperate figure leading lurid charges with one knee forward and a broken blade high - a blue, determined figure standing before a crimson and steel assault, getting calmly killed on a high place before the eyes of all. He thought of the magnificent pathos of his dead body. (p. 127)

Describe daydream heroics.

(8)

A tree feels pain to whimsy's strain.

The Return of the Native

Each stem was wrenched at the root, where it moved like a bone in its socket, and at every onset of the gale convulsive sounds came from the branches, as if pain were felt. (p. 247)

Describe trees applauding on a breezy day.

(9)

Fantasies approach,
Flags counsel and coach.

The Great Gatsby

"I was walking along from one place to another, half on the sidewalks and half on the lawns...I had on a new plaid skirt also that blew a little in the wind, and whenever this happened the red, white, and blue banners in front of all the houses stretched out stiff and said tut-tut-tut-tut, in a disapproving way." (p. 75)

Describe what a locker, book, or car has to say to its user.

(10)

Flowers with eyes? Floral spies!

Silas Marner

It'll be a deal livelier at the Stone-pits when we've got some flowers, for I always think the flowers can see us, and know what we're talking about. (p. 175)

Describe the thoughts of a rose as someone appears with garden shears!

STUDY HINTS

Do your own work. Remember, you have personal ideas
to put down and so does everyone else. Above all, do not
borrow from a quoted passage.

Before you start, think through these words:

Nouns	Verbs	Adjectives	Adverbs
daydream	appear as if	curious	audibly
exaggeration	escape	dreamlike	believably
fascination	go in thought	enchanting	dreamily
nightmare	make believe	freeing	incredibly
notion	picture	illusive	innocently
vision	pretend	romantic	seemingly
whim	wish	whimsical	visually

While working, turn to dictionaries for exact meanings
and search in a synonym dictionary (thesaurus) for better
words.

Before reading your finished product aloud, rehearse it
until it sounds good. Read the way you talk only a bit slower
and louder, remembering to pause between groups of ideas so
everyone will "get it."

Begin most sentences low and smoothly raise the pitch to
hit each word expressing a new idea. Practice reading this
while moving your lips: "Suddenly like a <u>bolt</u> out of the red,
white, and <u>blue</u>, the flags were <u>speaking</u>!"

"Good readers make good writers."

CHAPTER 14. RELATIONSHIP PASSAGES

Family and friends, females and males,
To your side of the court the ball sails.

Choose a couple of assignments and write 30-70 words each. Check out the study hints for this chapter (page eighty-four).

(1)

I've cut my ties with everyone.
Society for me is over and done.
No more partners, don't be stunned.
Forget it! I'd rather be gunned!

Victory

He meant to drift altogether and literally, body and soul, like a detached leaf drifting in the wind-currents under the immovable trees of a forest glade; to drift without ever catching on to anything. (p. 92)

Describe a high schooler who prefers to do things alone.

(2)

He wants acceptance from his peers,
But his strangeness interferes.

Brave New World

The mockery made him feel an outsider; and feeling an outsider he behaved like one, which increased the prejudice against him and intensified the contempt and hostility aroused by his physical defects. Which in turn increased his sense of being alien and alone. (p. 43)

Describe prejudice against a particular person.

(3)

Kicked out of school,
Playing it cool.
Troubled for another,
Troubled about mother.

The Catcher in the Rye

She hasn't felt too healthy since my brother Allie died. She's very nervous. That's another reason why I hated like hell for her to know I got the ax again. (p. 140)

Describe a student breaking the news about being cut from a group activity at school.

(4)

Tommy, paroled from prison,
Comes home from across state.
His mother's hopes have risen,
And his, reciprocate.

The Grapes of Wrath

She moved toward him lithely, soundlessly in her bare feet, and her face was full of wonder. Her small hand felt his arm, felt the soundness of his muscles. And then her fingers went up to his cheek as a blind man's fingers might. And her joy was nearly like sorrow. Tom pulled his underlip between his teeth and bit it. Her eyes went wonderingly to his bitten lip, and she saw the little line of blood against his teeth and the trickle of blood down his lip. Then she knew, and her control came back, and her hand dropped. Her breath came out explosively. (p. 96)

Describe a greeting after a trip away from home.

(5)

Young boy shivers nonplussed
In river swift and swirling,
Water deep and hair-curling.
His uncle he never will trust.

Black Boy

Whenever I saw his face the memory of my terror upon the river would come back, vivid and strong, and it stood as a barrier between us. (p. 62)

Discuss someone losing trust in a brother or sister.

(6)

Two are the women who bring him up.
Of his interest they'll not sup;
At their church he'll not perch.
He feels betrayed, left in lurch.

Black Boy

Granny and Aunt Addie changed toward me, giving me up for lost; they told me that they were dead to the world, and those of their blood who lived in that world were therefore dead to them. From urgent solicitude they dropped to coldness and hostility. (p. 135)

Discuss tension in a household over poor grades or future plans.

(7)

He couldn't love both of us, could he?
We have a problem, so does Dunwoodie!
Hard to untangle a triangle.

The Spy

"Do you know Dunwoodie? Have you seen him often?"

Once more Frances ventured to look her guest in the face, and again she met the piercing eyes bent on her, as if to search her inmost heart. (p. 148)

> Describe a meeting between two guys who find they both are dating the same "chick."

(8)

She's an earth angel, he's completely convinced.
She's the soul mate he's up against.

Green Mansions

Still, in some mysterious way, Rima had become to me...a being apart and sacred, and this feeling seemed to mix with my passion, to purify and exalt it and make it infinitely sweet and precious. (p. 149)

> Describe a high schooler who's "got it bad!"

(9)

Both people know
When a breakup comes.
It's written in the air,
It's history, it's not fair.

Jane Eyre

...as long as he and I lived he never would forget them. I saw by his look, when he turned to me, that they were always written on the air between me and him; whenever I spoke, they sounded in my voice to his ear; and their echo toned every answer he gave me. (p. 457)

Describe a couple splitting up.

(10)

Enemy is friend
Seeking out sin,
Not to mend but rend.
A cruel game to be in.

The Scarlet Letter

He now dug into the poor clergyman's heart, like a miner searching for gold; or, rather, like a sexton delving into a grave, possibly in quest of a jewel that had been buried on the dead man's bosom, but likely to find nothing save mortality and corruption. (p. 93)

Describe someone who taunts a friend about something he'd like to forget.

STUDY HINTS

Do your own work. Remember, you have personal ideas to put down and so does everyone else. Above all, do not borrow from a quoted passage.

Before you start, think through these words:

Nouns	Verbs	Adjectives	Adverbs
affection	abuse	alone	genuinely
barrier	criticize	burdened	icily
betrayal	favor	cold-hearted	insincerely
mask	link	mellow	sweetly
outsider	reject	nagging	tactfully
rival	scoff	stiff-necked	tenderly
sorrow	toy with	uneasy	trustfully

While working, turn to dictionaries for exact meanings and search in a synonym dictionary (thesaurus) for better words.

Before reading your finished product aloud, rehearse it until it sounds good. Read the way you talk only a bit slower and louder, remembering to pause between groups of ideas so everyone will "get it."

Begin most sentences low and smoothly raise the pitch to hit each word expressing a new idea. Practice reading this while moving your lips: "He asked again and again, finally punishing her for defying him."

"Good readers make good writers."

CHAPTER 15. TRAGIC TONES

Give us grief now without fear.
Don't be brief, let us hear.

Accept a couple of suggestions and write 30-70 words each.
Check out the study hints for this chapter (page ninety).

(1)

Some folks have no children to see.
Children seem fated never to be.

My Antonia

Otto was already one of those drifting, case-hardened labourers who never marry or have children of their own. Yet he was so fond of children! (p. 70)

Describe the feelings of someone who never knew a parent or brother or sister.

(2)

Frustrated dreams, black magic,
Too poor to marry is tragic.

The Jungle

But day by day the music of Tamoszius's violin became more passionate and heart-breaking, and Marija would sit with her hands clasped and her cheeks wet and all her body atremble, hearing in the wailing melodies the voices of the unborn generations which cried out in her for life. (p. 108)

Describe a boyfriend or girlfriend moving to a distant locality.

(3)

White fluffy poodle dies;
Child is floored.
Tragedy meets eyes;
Can't be ignored.

Black Boy

A week later Betsy was crushed to death beneath the wheels of a coal wagon. I cried and buried her in the back yard and drove a barrel staving into the ground at the head of her grave. (p. 81)

Describe a child's first taste of death.

(4)

Solitary weaver not consoled.
Gone is solace and hard-earned gold.

Silas Marner

And all the evening, as he sat in his loneliness by his dull fire, he leaned his elbows on his knees, and clasped his head with his hands, and moaned very low - not as one who seeks to be heard. (p. 97)

Describe feelings at the loss of a prized possession.

(5)

Minister travels to sister,
Leading life unclean.
Her shame, his forgiveness,
A touching scene.

Cry, the Beloved Country

I do not like Johannesburg, she says. She looks at him with eyes of distress, and his heart quickens with hope. I am a bad woman, my brother. I am no woman to go back.

His eyes fill will tears, his deep gentleness returns to him. He goes to her and lifts her from the floor to the chair. Inarticulately he strokes her face, his heart filled with pity. (p. 31)

Describe kindness towards someone in need of forgiveness.

(6)

War represents madness, wall-to-wall badness.
A grim, shocking affair that gets nowhere.

The Jungle

"We call it War, and pass it by...come with me, come with me - <u>realize it!</u> See the bodies of men pierced by bullets, blown into pieces by bursting shells! Hear the crunching of the bayonet, plunged into human flesh; hear the groans and shrieks of agony, see the faces of men crazed by pain, turned into fiends by fury and hate! Put your hand upon that piece of flesh - it is hot and quivering - just now it was a part of a man! This blood is still steaming - it was driven by a human heart! Almighty God! and this goes on - it is systematic, organized, premeditated!" (p. 300)

Describe a war newscast.

(7)

Soldier boy completed rest.
On to war front, leaving nest.
Porter's wife starts crying, unhappy.
Why should she becomes sappy?

A Farewell to Arms

I patted her on the back and she cried once more. She had done my mending and was a very short dumpy, happy-faced woman with white hair. When she cried her whole face went to pieces. (p. 146)

Describe someone who suddenly fears for the safety of someone starting off.

(8)

In times of illness we try to be brave.
An act of kindness can make us cave.

The Grapes of Wrath

He looked up at her, drawn by her soft voice. "Come over now," she said. "You'll git some rest. We'll he'p you over."
    Without warning Grampa began to cry. His chin wavered and his old lips tightened over his mouth and he sobbed hoarsely. (p. 173)

Describe reactions by old or poor to offers of help.

(9)

Leper deserted the army;
Now his looks alarm me.
The more his mind's all thumbs,
The queerer his laugh becomes.

A Separate Peace

"That's too bad," the strained laughter was back in his voice, "Snow White with Brinker's face on her. There's a picture," then he broke into sobs. (p. 140)

Describe how a child feels when realizing a grandparent no longer recognizes him or her.

(10)

Bitten by mad dog,
Her husband crazy as well.
His sickness goes whole hog,
A tragedy to tell.

Their Eyes Were Watching God

She saw him coming from the outhouse with a queer loping gait, swinging his head from side to side and his jaws clenched in a funny way. This was too awful! (p. 174)

Describe someone out of control due to an illness, drugs, or alcohol.

STUDY HINTS

Do your own work. Remember, you have personal ideas to put down and so does everyone else. Above all, do not borrow from a quoted passage.

Before you start, think through these words:

Nouns	Verbs	Adjectives	Adverbs
bad dream	agonize	courageous	fatally
defeat	face	disappointed	feebly
end	fight on	forlorn	heroically
shadow	give up	grim	never
struggle	overwhelm	hideous	unluckily
trial	sigh	outmatched	unthinkably
unfortunate	wail	stricken	vainly

While working, turn to dictionaries for exact meanings and search in a synonym dictionary (thesaurus) for better words.

Before reading your finished product aloud, rehearse it until it sounds good. Read the way you talk only a bit slower and louder, remembering to pause between groups of ideas so everyone will "get it."

Begin most sentences low and smoothly raise the pitch to hit each word expressing a new idea. Practice reading this while moving your lips: "He will never forgive himself for mistreating her so."

"Good readers make good writers."

CHAPTER 16. COMIC TONES

With the comic muse break bread,
Start hopeful...finish ahead!

Accept a couple of jobs and write 30-70 words each.
Check out the study hints for this chapter (page ninety-six).

(1)

Deliver the line that's witty;
It's "Hey, lighten up!" city.

To Kill a Mockingbird

"Yes sir, but - "
"Well, you're in trouble now. Stay there."
...I turned to flee but Uncle Jack was quicker. I found myself suddenly look-ing at a tiny ant struggling with a bread crumb in the grass. (p. 93)

Describe someone telling a story on himself or herself.

(2)

When heaviness is a drag,
Drag out the sight gag.

The Adventures of Huckleberry Finn

My heart fell down amongst my lungs and livers and things, and a hard piece of corn-crust started down my throat after it and got met on the road with a cough, and was shot across the table, and took one of the children in the eye and curled him up like a fishing-worm, and let a cry out of him the size of a war-whoop. (p. 226)

Describe an embarrassing accident at mealtime.

(3)

Tinge of cartoon in our behalf,
Scrunch of smile, wide-open laugh.

Sherlock Holmes

...smiling in the most pleasant fashion until his eyes were just two little slits amid the white creases of his face...
He leaned back in his chair and laughed his eyes into his head again. (p. 319)

> Describe comically a mouth opening wide and clamping shut.

(4)

A comic face peps up a story.
Relax, it's self-explanatory.

Light in August

He said she was just tall enough to see over the counter, so that she didn't look like she had any body at all. It just looked like somebody had sneaked up and set a toy balloon with a face painted on it and a comic hat set on top of it, like the Katzenjammer kids in the funny paper. (p. 310)

> Write a verbal cartoon about someone losing balance and taking a fall.

(5)

Eyes set close together
Get their act together.

A Tale of Two Cities

"He will then let you in."
"Into the court, sir?"
"Into the court."
Mr. Cruncher's eyes seemed to get a little closer to one another, and to
interchange the inquiry, "What do you think of this?" (p. 73)

Describe gossip causing eyes to communicate.

(6)

Harshly called to explain
A doubtful laundry count.
Loathly he moves with strain,
Nurse's stare to surmount.

One Flew Over the Cuckoo's Nest

He puts his hands in his pockets and starts shuffling down the hall to
her...all the hate and fury and frustration she was planning to use on
McMurphy is beaming out down the hall at the black boy, and he can
feel it blast against him like a blizzard wind, slowing him more than
ever. He has to lean into it, pulling his arms around him. Frost forms in
his hair and eyebrows. He leans farther forward, but his steps are get-
ting slower; he'll never make it. (p. 88)

Describe an encounter with fiery glares.

(7)

Language horseplay and fractured facts.
Logic, gangway! Grammar gets the ax!

The Adventures of Huckleberry Finn

...Uncle Silas he had a noble brass warming-pan which he thought considerable of, because it belonged to one of his ancestors with a long wooden handle that come over from England with William the Conqueror in the Mayflower *or one of them early ships and was hid away up garret with a lot of other old pots and things that was valuable. (p. 230)*

Describe a subject with "screwed-up" phrases and clauses.

(8)

Inventing terms unaware, syllable by syllable,
Can be a bear or really quite thrillable.

The Adventures of Huckleberry Finn

It was pretty ornery preaching - all about brotherly love, and such-like tiresomeness; but everybody said it was a good sermon, and they all talked it over going home, and had such a powerful lot to say about faith and good works and free grace and preforeordestination, and I don't know what all, that it did seem to me to be one of the roughest Sundays I had run across yet. (p. 98)

Invent a doubly long term and insert it into dialogue.

(9)

A battlefield doctor merry,
A walking, talking dictionary.

The Spy

"Bless me, what's that?" said Miss Peyton, turning pale at the report of the pistols fired at Birch.

"It sounds prodigiously like the concussion on the atmosphere made by the explosion of firearms," said the surgeon, sipping his tea with great indifference. (p. 92)

Describe the dialogue of a student whose language would indicate a recent visit to a dictionary.

(10)

We animals drove the farmers to town
With ideas to excite us.
But lately our leaders have come down
With committee-itis.

Animal Farm

Snowball also busied himself with organising the other animals into what he called Animal Committees. He was indefatigable at this. He formed the Egg Production Committee for the hens, the Clean Tails League for the cows, the Wild Comrades' Re-education Committee (the object of this was to tame the rats and rabbits), the Whiter Wool Movement for the sheep, and various others, besides instituting classes in reading and writing. (p. 39)

Describe unneeded committees designed for school.

STUDY HINTS

Do your own work. Remember, you have personal ideas to put down and so does everyone else. Above all, do not borrow from a quoted passage.

Before you start, think through these words:

Nouns	Verbs	Adjectives	Adverbs
amusement	banter	absurd	charmingly
clown	blunder	contagious	foolishly
game	explode	droll	humorously
grin	joke	embarrassing	impishly
prank	kid	goofy	laughingly
situation	quip	spontaneous	oddly
uproar	ridicule	surprising	suddenly

While working, turn to dictionaries for exact meanings and search in a synonym dictionary (thesaurus) for better words.

Before reading your finished product aloud, rehearse it until it sounds good. Read the way you talk only a bit slower and louder, remembering to pause between groups of ideas so everyone will "get it."

Begin most sentences low and smoothly raise the pitch to hit each word expressing a new idea. Practice reading this while moving your lips: "Duffy is so confused he loses his balance and falls off the platform."

   "Good readers make good writers."

CHAPTER 17. TENSION AND SUSPENSE

Be yourself and not your mama.
Grip us with nail-biting drama.

Choose a couple of exercises and write 30-70 words each.
Check out the study hints for this chapter (page 102).

(1)

Confrontation stimulates prose,
Faces pale white or deep rose.

Light in August

Their faces were not a foot apart: the one cold, dead white, fanatical, mad; the other parchment-colored, the lip lifted into the shape of a soundless and rigid snarl. (p. 242)

Describe faces in an "in-your-face" argument.

(2)

White-knuckle fish story,
Man-versus-beast category.

The Old Man and the Sea

He felt faint again now but he held on the great fish all the strain that he could. I moved him, he thought. Maybe this time I can get him over. Pull, hands, he thought. Hold up, legs. Last for me, head. Last for me. (p. 91)

Describe someone talking to his body during a sports event or workout.

(3)

An intruder entered,
His target a pearl.
A knife jab centered,
Unnerving a girl.

The Pearl

Now the tension which had been growing in Juana boiled up to the surface and her lips were thin. "This thing is evil," she cried harshly. "This pearl is like a sin! It will destroy us," and her voice rose shrilly. (p. 50)

Describe words spoken in relief, anger, or fear after a close call.

(4)

Life in prison is dreary.
Of questions he is weary.
He has nothing further to give.
His crime they make him relive.

Cry, the Beloved Country

Or does he weep for himself alone, to be let be, to be let alone, to be free of the merciless rain of questions, why, why, why, when he knows not why. They do not speak with him, they do not jest with him, they do not sit and let him be, but they ask, ask, ask, why, why, why, - his father, the white man, the prison officers, the police, the magistrates, - why, why, why. (p. 99)

Describe the thoughts of a young person "grilled" by parents, teachers, etc.

(5)

Being a new kid at school,
I always feel a fool.
Learning to cope with fears,
I'm the target of my peers.

Black Boy

"Mama bought me a straw hat," he sneered.
"Watch what you're saying," I warned him.
"Oh, look! He talks!" the boy said.
The crowd howled with laughter, waiting, hoping. (p. 136)

Describe a tense moment in a school hall.

(6)

How, why, where?
Taste tension in the air.
Fateful letter of much import
In high drama read in court.

A Tale of Two Cities

In the dead silence and stillness - the prisoner under trial looked lovingly at
his wife, his wife only looking from him to look with solicitude at her father,
Dr. Manette keeping his eyes fixed on the reader, Madame Defarge never
taking hers from the prisoner, Defarge never taking his from his wife, and all
other eyes there intent upon the Doctor, who saw none of them - the paper
was read as follows. (p. 405)

Describe the hush and attentiveness of the student body at
an assembly called by the principal or headmaster.

(7)

Mad dog holds people at bay;
Time seems to take all day.

To Kill a Mockingbird

In a fog, Jem and I watched our father take the gun and walk out into the middle of the street. He walked quickly, but I thought he moved like an underwater swimmer: time had slowed to a nauseating crawl. (p. 104)

Describe the sense of time when a car is spinning out of control.

(8)

Jurgis a midwife goes to fetch,
For his wife and baby.
The woman proceeds to hem and stretch.
Will she soon be ready? Maybe!

The Jungle

Then there was a black bonnet which had to be adjusted carefully, and an umbrella which was mislaid, and a bag full of necessities which had to be collected from here and there - the man being nearly crazy with anxiety in the meantime. (p. 184)

Describe impatiently waiting for someone to get ready to go out.

(9)

The stalkers are relaxed and slow,
Careful and deliberate.
Please may they hurry and go!

The Pearl

Kino was not breathing, but his back arched a little and the muscles of his arms and legs stood out with tension and a line of sweat formed on his upper lip. For a long moment the trackers bent over the road, and then they moved on slowly, studying the ground ahead of them, and the horseman moved after them. (p. 97)

Describe someone in hiding inside a house.

(10)

Prisoners stampede at door,
Trample each other on floor,
Despair for air and kin.
Survival instincts kick in.

Night

I could not answer him. Someone was lying full length on top of me, covering my face. I was unable to breathe, through either mouth or nose. Sweat beaded my brow, ran down my spine. This was the end - the end of the road. A silent death, suffocation. No way of crying out, of calling for help...

I succeeded in digging a hole through this wall of dying people, a little hole through which I could drink in a small quantity of air. (p. 89)

Describe feeling you are drowning.

STUDY HINTS

Do your own work. Remember, you have personal ideas to put down and so does everyone else. Above all, do not borrow from a quoted passage.

Before you start, think through these words:

Nouns	Verbs	Adjectives	Adverbs
breath	choose	edgy	anxiously
escape	inch along	faint	crucially
jam	lurk	frozen	deceptively
snare	panic	nail-biting	desperately
strain	pause	pressured	intently
sweat	slow	time	relentlesslly
trick	threaten	taut	watchfully

While working, turn to dictionaries for exact meanings and search in a synonym dictionary (thesaurus) for better words.

Before reading your finished product aloud, rehearse it until it sounds good. Read the way you talk only a bit slower and louder, remembering to pause between groups of ideas so everyone will "get it."

Begin most sentences low and smoothly raise the pitch to hit each word expressing a new idea. Practice reading this while moving your lips: "He feels that everyone is laughing at his appearance."

"Good readers make good writers."

CHAPTER 18. TIME ELEMENTS

Time is passing, time is ducking.
Write your words, keep on trucking.

Accept a couple of tasks and write 30-70 words each.
Check out the study hints for this chapter (page 108).

(1)

Time affects us all and all our things.
To cars and stars influence it brings.

The Grapes of Wrath

His gray cap was so new that the visor was still stiff and the button still on, not shapeless and bulged as it would be when it had served for a while all the various purposes of a cap - carrying sack, towel, handkerchief. (p. 9)

Describe a new belonging in terms of what it will become over time.

(2)

While we wait, time hushes.
When on the move, it rushes.

The Red Badge of Courage

The regiment, unmolested as yet, awaited the moment when the gray shadows of the woods before them should be slashed by the lines of flame. (p. 184)

Describe killing time while waiting for something to happen.

(3)

Use a watch or clock
Or in the sun take stock.

Of Mice and Men

At about ten o'clock in the morning the sun threw a bright dust-laden bar through one of the side windows, and in and out of the beam flies shot like rushing stars. (p. 17)

Describe a time of night in terms of traffic, lights, and moon.

(4)

When breezes slow and shadows lengthen,
Time pauses, calm and quiet strengthen.

Of Mice and Men

George stacked the scattered cards and began to lay out his solitaire hand. The shoes thudded on the ground outside. At the windows the light of the evening still made the window squares bright. (p. 40)

Describe a break towards the end of the day.

(5)

Time, rate, and distance hover
While captain races for cover.

The Sea Wolf

His whole concern was with the immediate, objective present. He still held the wheel, and I felt that he was timing Time, reckoning the passage of the minutes with each forward lunge and leeward roll of the Ghost. (p. 166)

Describe someone on the move planning and measuring time.

(6)

Time for leisure, time on your hands?
Time never waits when duty demands.

Sherlock Holmes

We heard the steps of our visitors descend the stair and the bang of the front door. In an instant Holmes had changed from the languid dreamer to the man of action. (p. 689)

Describe a high schooler changing from relaxation to action.

(7)
Is this a one-shot affair?
Or like combing hair?

My Antonia

As they went up the hill he kept glancing at her sidewise, to see whether she got his point, or how she received it. I noticed later that he always looked at people sidewise, as a work-horse does at its yokemate. (p. 278)

> Describe a person's odd movement, expression, or phrase that turns out to be a habit.

(8)
Tire mark and broken post,
A mishap's certain ghost.

The Red Badge of Courage

The men saw a ground vacant of fighters. It would have been an empty stage if it were not for a few corpses that lay thrown and twisted into fantastic shapes upon the sward. (p. 226)

> Describe evidence of a recent event.

(9)

A calendar is a schedule slick,
But a family has a yardstick,
Its very own red-letter date
When time and memory associate.

The Pearl

This was to be the day from which all other days would take their arrangement. Thus they would say, "It was two years before we sold the pearl," or, "It was six weeks after we sold the pearl." (p. 56)

Describe a family event that governs a collective memory.

(10)

Wouldn't it be swell
To lock the world away in jell,
To always read the finest page
Of life at just your age?

The Catcher in the Rye

Certain things they should stay the way they are. You ought to be able to stick them in one of those big glass cases and just leave them alone. I know that's impossible, but it's too bad anyway. (p. 158)

Describe a desire to freeze time at one or another stage in life.

STUDY HINTS

Do your own work. Remember, you have personal ideas
to put down and so does everyone else. Above all, do not
borrow from a quoted passage.

Before you start, think through these words:

Nouns	Verbs	Adjectives	Adverbs
change	drag	boring	before
dawn	expect	daily	eventually
evening	finish	dismal	instantly
milestone	march	fleeting	later
stream	pave the way	regrettable	longingly
wait	rush	renewed	repeatedly
watershed	start	spontaneous	temporarily

While working, turn to dictionaries for exact meanings
and search in a synonym dictionary (thesaurus) for better
words.

Before reading your finished product aloud, rehearse it
until it sounds good. Read the way you talk only a bit slower
and louder, remembering to pause between groups of ideas so
everyone will "get it."

Begin most sentences low and smoothly raise the pitch to
hit each word expressing a new idea. Practice reading this
while moving your lips: "Before they emerge from the cave,
we are aware of the measured passage of time."

"Good readers make good writers."

CHAPTER 19. RHYTHM WRITING

The pulse of language, yes,
It's natural to express.

Accept a couple of chores and write 30-70 words each.
Check out the study hints for this chapter (page 114).

(1)

Adam, face to soil, back to sky,
Is joined by Eve by and by.

The Good Earth

Moving together in a perfect rhythm, without a word, hour after hour, he fell into a union with her which took the pain from his labor. (p. 22)

Describe the coordination of a pair of dancers, skaters, etc.

(2)

The drudge of a human robot:
Pity his kind, pity a lot.

The Jungle

Hour after hour, day after day, year after year, it was fated that he should stand upon a certain square foot of floor from seven in the morning until noon, and again from half-past twelve till half-past five, making never a motion and thinking never a thought, save for the setting of lard cans. (p. 75)

Describe the beat of a boring task.

(3)

The sleeping sea's rocking sighs,
Pausing and heaving under blue skies,
Replace breakers and sprays,
Tangling guys, sheets, and stays.

The Sea Wolf

Her task was to hold the boat in position while I worked at the tangle. And such a tangle - halyards, sheets, guys, downhauls, shrouds, stays, and all washed about and back and forth and through, and twined and knotted by the sea. (p. 219)

Describe objects blown about by the wind.

(4)

Take as another fork
Crosscurrents with bobbing cork.
Back and forth, up and down,
As funny as a clown.

The Keys of the Kingdom

Together, not speaking, cut by the wind, they stood watching the far circle of corks dancing in the choppy back-lash where the river met the sea. (p. 14)

Describe the motion of water in a crowded pool.

(5)

Sound-and-light weather show
Seen from cave above the flow.
Cymbals and guns of thunder
Strike the mind with wonder.

The Adventures of Huckleberry Finn

It was one of these regular summer storms. It would get so dark that it looked all blue-black outside, and lovely; and the rain would thrash along by so thick that the trees off a little ways looked dim and spider-webby; and there would come a blast of wind that would bend the trees down and turn up the pale underside of the leaves; and then a perfect ripper of a gust would follow along and set the branches to tossing their arms as if they was just wild; and next, when it was just about the bluest and blackest -fst! it was as bright as glory, and you'd have a little glimpse of treetops a-plunging about away off yonder in the storm, hundreds of yards further than you could see before; dark as sin again in a second, and now you'd hear the thunder let go with an awful crash, and then go rumbling, grumbling, tumbling, down the sky towards the under side of the world, like rolling empty barrels downstairs - where it's long stairs and they bounce a good deal, you know. (p. 43)

Describe a storm from the viewpoint of one caught out in it.

(6)

After a downpour coasts to an end,
Dripping droplets and silence blend.

Lord of the Flies

Then the breeze died too and there was no noise save the drip and trickle of water that ran out of clefts and spilled down, leaf by leaf, to the brown earth of the island. (p. 139)

Describe the movement of a ride slowing to a stop.

(7)

Repeating a phrase, just as it was,
Drives the point home, yes it does!

For Whom the Bell Tolls

How many times had he heard this? How many times had he watched people say it with difficulty? How many times had he seen their eyes fill and their throats harden with the difficulty of saying my father, or my brother, or my mother, or my sister? He could not remember how many times he had heard them mention their dead in this way. (p. 134)

Use the phrase "how long before..." repeated in a statement.

(8)

As certain as smoke will rise,
As certain as a hound's prize.

The Scarlet Letter

"It irks me, nevertheless, that the partner of her iniquity should not, at least, stand on the scaffold by her side. But he will be known! - he will be known! - he will be known!" (p. 50)

Use the phrase "but we will win!" repeated in a statement.

(9)

Guitar strum or native drum,
Spastic tumble or engine rumble,
Heart beats...and beats...and beats.

Heart of Darkness

And I remember I confounded the beat of the drum with the beating of my heart, and was pleased at its calm regularity. (p. 142)

Describe an excited heart beating in time with fast-approaching footsteps.

(10)

Madame Defarge, her hate fulfilling,
Foretells revenge and guillotine killing.

A Tale of Two Cities

She stood immovable close to the grim old officer, and remained close to him; remained immovable close to him through the streets...remained immovable close to him when he was got near his destination, and began to be struck at from behind; remained immovable close to him when the long-gathering rain of stabs and blows fell heavy; was so close to him when he dropped dead under it, that, suddenly animated, she put her foot upon his neck, and with her cruel knife - long ready - hewed off his head. (p. 278)

Using the phrase "close to" repeatedly, describe an athlete closely guarding an opponent before making a move.

STUDY HINTS

Do your own work. Remember, you have personal ideas to put down and so does everyone else. Above all, do not borrow from a quoted passage.

Before you start, think through these words:

Nouns	Verbs	Adjectives	Adverbs
heartbeats	cycle	choppy	in sync
humming	fade	clock-like	musically
mounting	pause	mechanical	over again
pulse	repeat	non-pausing	quietly
surge	sing	rapid	suddenly
tune	soar	rocky	toddling
wave	tumble	rousing	together

While working, turn to dictionaries for exact meanings and search in a synonym dictionary (thesaurus) for better words.

Before reading your finished product aloud, rehearse it until it sounds good. Read the way you talk only a bit slower and louder, remembering to pause between groups of ideas so everyone will "get it."

Begin most sentences low and smoothly raise the pitch to hit each word expressing a new idea. Practice reading this while moving your lips: "We tap our feet to the brisk flow of the English language."

"Good readers make good writers."

CHAPTER 20. COMPARISON COUPLES

Keep chugging, keep plugging,
Cope with comparisons.

Accept a couple of challenges and write 30-70 words each.
Check out the study hints for this chapter (page 120).

(1)

Neat parallel short and sweet,
Carefree in tone, graceful treat.

The Great Gatsby

At 158th Street the cab stopped at one slice in a long white cake of apartment houses. (p. 28)

Compare three people together to a sandwich.

(2)

A razzle-dazzle hot-roll mention
Like a loud commercial grabs attention.

Victory

Behind his back the sun, touching the water, was like a disc of iron cooled to a dull red glow, ready to start rolling round the circular steel plate of sea, which, under the darkening sky, looked more solid than the high ridge of Samburan... (p. 235)

Compare cars on a highway to buns moving through a bakery.

(3)

News to a dead-beat dad,
Shocked to the spine.
Blood rushes from his face;
A giveaway sign!

Light in August

*Lena on the cot watched the white scar beside his mouth vanish completely,
as if the ebb of blood behind it had snatched the scar in passing like a rag
from a clothesline. (p. 376)*

Compare a departing crowd to words deleted on a computer screen.

(4)

Missionary priest plays with notion,
Distance to go like Atlantic Ocean.

The Keys of the Kingdom

*Momentarily, the seismograph of his mind faintly registered the shock: a
glimmering of the knowledge of the incomprehensibility of God...We are like
tiny ants in a bottomless abyss, covered with a million layers of cotton wool,
striving...to see the sky. (p. 141)*

Compare people to bees.

(5)

Demoted, grounded, what is the rule?
From exotic to common, let me see.
Ah...a human hummingbird is cool!
An apt and convincing analogy.

Green Mansions

Have you ever observed a humming bird moving about in an aerial dance among the flowers...how in turning it catches the sunshine...? And have you seen this same fairy-like creature suddenly perch itself on a twig, in the shade, its misty wings and fanlike tail folded, the iridescent glory vanished, looking like some common dull-plumaged little bird sitting listless in a cage? Just so great was the difference in the girl, as I had seen her in the forest and as she now appeared under the smoky roof in the fire-light. (p. 79)

Compare maintaining a friendship with holding a bird gently.

(6)

Joe plans an escape one night,
From mean stepparents his flight.
A sober statement no doubt
Requires a boost to bring it about.

Light in August

When he went to bed that night his mind was made up to run away. He felt like an eagle: hard, sufficient, potent, remorseless, strong. But that passed, though he did not then know that, like the eagle, his own flesh as well as all space was still a cage. (p. 140)

Compare someone growing up to a bird pecking open its shell and flying away.

(7)

Ship hell-bent and flush
With tubs of molten blubber,
In devil-may-care rush
Not captained by landlubber.

Moby Dick

...the rushing Pequod, freighted with savages, and laden with fire, and burning a corpse, and plunging into that darkness of darkness, seemed the material counterpart of her monomaniac commander's soul. (p. 421)

> Describe a person out of control who resembles a car or truck out of control.

(8)

Rebecca, spirit on rise,
Listens to accuser's lies.
To prove she is no witch,
She raises the stakes a pitch.

Ivanhoe

"Seest thou, Rebecca, as this thin and light glove of thine is to one of our heavy steel gauntlets, so is thy cause to that of the Temple."
"Cast my innocence into the scale," answered Rebecca, "and the glove of silk shall outweigh the glove of iron." (p. 406)

> Compare a dispute to a tug of war.

(9)

Scent flavors and skin knobs
At the stereoscopic feelies.
A last kiss like a dying moth,
For the customer's ease.

Brave New World

Then the bearskin made a final appearance and, amid a blare of sexophones, the last stereoscopic kiss faded into darkness, the last electric titillation died on the lips like a dying moth that quivers, quivers, ever more feebly, ever more faintly, and at last is quiet, quite still. (p. 114)

Compare a hug to a handshake.

(10)

An upset gal with crying need
Surrenders to a pitying guy,
Who holds and pats, takes the lead.
Like injured bird she has her cry.

The Keys of the Kingdom

The racking violence of her sobs diminished gradually. She was like a wounded bird in his arms... (p. 74)

Compare a laugh to a bird cry.

STUDY HINTS

Do your own work. Remember, you have personal ideas to put down and so does everyone else. Above all, do not borrow from a quoted passage.

Before you start, think through these words:

Nouns	Verbs	Adjectives	Adverbs
hint	agree	apparent	clearly
image	be like	echoing	equally
imitation	copy	identical	exactly
likeness	look as if	no different	in common
message	match	parallel	in look
mirror	mimic	resembling	likewise
symbol	seem	surprising	similarly

While working, turn to dictionaries for exact meanings and search in a synonym dictionary (thesaurus) for better words.

Before reading your finished product aloud, rehearse it until it sounds good. Read the way you talk only a bit slower and louder, remembering to pause between groups of ideas so everyone will "get it."

Begin most sentences low and smoothly raise the pitch to hit each word expressing a new idea. Practice reading this while moving your lips: "The green spring is the morning, the yellow summer the afternoon, the brown fall the evening, and the dark winter the night."

"Good readers make good writers."

CHAPTER 21. ACCURACY COUNTS

Youth can't limit
Your storytelling truth.

Choose a couple of activities and write 30-70 words each. Check out the study hints for this chapter (page 126).

(1)

Design and location pin it down.
An eye for detail, why the frown?

A Farewell to Arms

"How many times have you been wounded, Ettore?"
"Three times bad. I got three wound stripes. See?" He pulled his sleeve around. The strips were parallel silver lines on a black background sewed to the cloth of the sleeve about eight inches below the shoulder. (p. 121)

Describe the design and location of a logo or label on clothing.

(2)

A window store display
Telling it the basic way.

A Farewell to Arms

We were standing in front of the leather goods shop. There were riding boots, a rucksack and ski boots in the window. Each article was set apart as an exhibit; the rucksack in the centre, the riding boots on one side and the ski boots on the other. (p. 147)

Describe a table set for dinner.

(3)

Describe a house, describe a barn,
Picture a street, spin a yarn.

Silas Marner

The greatest man in Raveloe was Squire Cass, who lived in the large red house with the handsome flight of stone steps in front and the high stables behind it, nearly opposite the church. (p. 25)

> Describe the exact location of a particular house or business.

(4)

Set the tone, set the stage.
Describe numbers, directions, lighting,
People too, no matter the age.
Everyone ready? Continue writing!

The Time Machine

He took one of the small octagonal tables that were scattered about the room, and set it in front of the fire, with two legs on the hearthrug. On this table he placed the mechanism. Then he drew up a chair, and sat down. The only other object on the table was a small shaded lamp, the bright light of which fell upon the model. There were also perhaps a dozen candles about, two in brass candlesticks upon the mantel and several in sconces, so that the room was brilliantly illuminated. I sat in a low arm-chair nearest the fire, and I drew this forward so as to be almost between the Time Traveler and the fireplace. Filby sat behind him, looking over his shoulder. The Medical Man and the Provincial Mayor watched him in profile from the right, the Psychologist from the left. The Very Young Man stood behind the Psychologist. We were all on the alert. (p. 13)

> Describe placement of furniture, lighting, and people gathered in a classroom or in a room at home.

(5)

Step by step, an orderly flow.
A sequence of movements, then go!

The Return of the Native

At half-past eleven, finding that the house was silent, Eustacia had lighted her candle, put on some warm outer wrappings, taken her bag in her hand, and, extinguishing the light again, descended the staircase. (p. 420)

Describe the steps you might take to leave the house.

(6)

Moist breath on cold pane,
A mosaic of features for the brain.

Orient Express

...a mist from his breath obscured the pane, so that soon he could see of those who passed no more than unrelated features, a peering angry eye, a dress of mauve silk, a clerical collar. (p. 16)

Describe what comes through when a bathroom mirror is partly fogged over.

(7)

Info is major, detail is right.
Dust and fuzz - what a sight!

A Separate Peace

The light should have been off. Instead, as though alive itself, it poured in a thin yellow slab of brightness from under the door, illuminating the dust and splinters of the hall floor. (p. 94)

Describe what lies about undisturbed on a bare floor.

(8)

Eyes teared and body trembled,
Piggy spoke words
To friends assembled,
Faithful watchwords.

Lord of the Flies

Piggy ended, flushed and trembling. He pushed the conch quickly into Ralph's hands as though in a hurry to be rid of it and wiped the tears from his eyes. The green light was gentle about them and the conch lay at Ralph's feet, fragile and white. A single drop of water that had escaped Piggy's fingers now flashed on the delicate curve like a star. (p. 156)

Describe drops of perspiration on a face or body.

(9)

Billboards, bumper stickers, T-shirt tricks.
A talent for detail just for kicks.

The Catcher in the Rye

There was this empty box of Kolynos toothpaste outside Leahy and Hoffman's door, and while I walked down towards the stairs, I kept giving it a boot with this sheeplined slipper I had on. (p. 66)

Describe objects stepped on, walked over or around, or kicked.

(10)

For graphic prose on the nose,
Use picture speech that knows.

Fahrenheit 451

The books leapt and danced like roasted birds, their wings ablaze with red and yellow feathers. (p. 127)

Using a comparison, describe how something burns or cooks.

STUDY HINTS

Do your own work. Remember, you have personal ideas to put down and so does everyone else. Above all, do not borrow from a quoted passage.

Before you start, think through these words:

Nouns	Verbs	Adjectives	Adverbs
center	concentrate	close-up	after
detail	notice	eagle-sighted	behind
dimensions	observe	exact	carefully
eyewitness	outline	how many	in front
focus	pinpoint	loud and clear	near
measure	spell out	opposite	next to
side	target	sharp	precisely

While working, turn to dictionaries for exact meanings and search in a synonym dictionary (thesaurus) for better words.

Before reading your finished product aloud, rehearse it until it sounds good. Read the way you talk only a bit slower and louder, remembering to pause between groups of ideas so everyone will "get it."

Begin most sentences low and smoothly raise the pitch to hit each word expressing a new idea. Practice reading this while moving your lips: "A scar-nosed <u>athlete</u> has a contagious <u>laugh</u>."

"Good readers make good writers."

CHAPTER 22. CONTRAST HIGHLIGHTS

Never say die!
Contrasts are minor miseries!
Choose a couple of assignments and write 30-70 words each. Check out the study hints for this chapter (page 132).

(1)
Hands and eyes both partake,
Eyes attentive, hands wide-awake.

A Tale of Two Cities

He then conducted the young lady straightway to her chair again, and, holding the chair-back with his left hand, and using his right by turns to rub his chin, pull his wig at the ears, or point what he said, stood looking down into her face while she sat looking up into his. (p. 29)

Describe hand motions of host or hostess seating a family at a restaurant.

(2)
A manly athlete in riding outfit,
Boots and coat a tight fit.

The Great Gatsby

Not even the effeminate swank of his riding clothes could hide the enormous power of that body - he seemed to fill those glistening boots until he strained the top lacing, and you could see a great pack of muscle shifting when his shoulder moved under his thin coat. (p. 7)

Describe a girl wearing a guy's shirt, sweater, or jacket.

(3)
Snowball, talker, gets his say.
Napoleon, silent, gets his way.

Animal Farm

Snowball was a more vivacious pig than Napoleon, quicker in speech and more inventive, but was not considered to have the same depth of character. (p. 25)

Contrast two high schoolers with different tendencies and reputations.

(4)
Seniors come to the dorm for roommates both:
Finny is warm, but Gene is loath.

A Separate Peace

Brinker and three cohorts came with much commotion into our room at 10:05 P.M. that night. "We're taking you out," he said flatly.

"It's after hours," I said; "Where?" said Finny with interest at the same time. (p. 156)

Contrast three different reactions when a movie is suggested.

(5)

Friendly sea on calm day:
Velvet paw, tranquil pr-r-r.
Angry sea on rough day:
Savage fang, fierce gr-r-r!

Moby Dick

At such times under an abated sun; afloat all day upon smooth, slow heaving swells; seated in his boat, light as a birch canoe; and so sociably mixing with the soft waves themselves, that like hearth-stone cats they purr against the gunwale; these are the times of dreamy quietude, when beholding the tranquil beauty and brilliancy of the ocean's skin, one forgets the tiger heart that pants beneath it; and would not willingly remember, that this velvet paw but conceals a remorseless fang. (p. 485)

Describe a sleeping dog as opposed to how he would act if disturbed by an intruder.

(6)

Scared dogs alight from train,
Someone in fact has been slain.
Each a well-trained hound,
Meek and shy, looks around.

Light in August

It halted only long enough to disgorge the two dogs: a thousand costly tons of intricate and curious metal glaring and crashing up and into an almost shocking silence filled with puny sounds of men, to vomit two gaunt and cringing phantoms whose droopeared and mild faces gazed with sad abjectness about at the wary, pale faces of men who had not slept very much. (p. 259)

Describe dogs barking around tractor, backhoe, or earth mover.

(7)

No one knows the couple's link;
Could this be hypocrisy's stink?

The Scarlet Letter

The sainted minister in the church! The woman of the scarlet letter in the market-place! What imagination would have been irreverent enough to surmise that the same scorching stigma was on them both? (p. 171)

> Describe high schoolers who keep their mutual fondness secret.

(8)

Organ grinder and monkey
Cheer outside of house.
Corpse in ancestral chair
Haunts inside of house.

The House of Seven Gables

To the common observer - who could understand nothing of the case, except the music and the sunshine on the hither side of the door - it might have been amusing to watch the pertinacity of the street performer...But to us, who know the inner heart of the Seven Gables as well as its exterior face, there is a ghastly effect in this repetition of light popular tunes at its doorstep. (p. 256)

> Describe someone feeling sad but acting cheerful.

(9)
He riles with blame,
She wild with shame.

The Jungle

She tried to get away, making him furious; he thought it was fear, or the pain of his clutch - he did not understand that it was the agony of her shame. (p. 151)

Describe a remark, laugh, or physical contact that someone takes the wrong way.

(10)
Scream of car
Heard from far.
Scream in car
Shouted and doubted.

Fahrenheit 451

...it was the open car and Mildred driving a hundred miles an hour across town...

"Keep it down to fifty-five, the minimum!" he shouted. "The what?" she shrieked. "Speed!" he shouted. And she pushed it up to one hundred and five miles an hour and tore the breath from his mouth. (p. 49)

Describe a player in a frenzied game hearing only part of his instructions and doing the wrong thing.

STUDY HINTS

Do your own work. Remember, you have personal ideas to put down and so does everyone else. Above all, do not borrow from a quoted passage.

Before you start, think through these words:

<u>Nouns</u>	<u>Verbs</u>	<u>Adjectives</u>	<u>Adverbs</u>
color	bury	beautiful-ugly	distinctly
conflict	clash	bogus-real	inwardly
difference	combine	caring-brutish	meekly
direction	expose	distant-mushy	publicly
gender	hide	puny-huge	outwardly
generation	mask	rich-penniless	privately
twist	reveal	strong-frail	smugly

While working, turn to dictionaries for exact meanings and search in a synonym dictionary (thesaurus) for better words.

Before reading your finished product aloud, rehearse it until it sounds good. Read the way you talk only a bit slower and louder, remembering to pause between groups of ideas so everyone will "get it."

Begin most sentences low and smoothly raise the pitch to hit each word expressing a new idea. Practice reading this while moving your lips: "Whenever we <u>study</u> a well-written <u>contrast</u>, writing skill may <u>improve</u>."

"Good readers make good writers."

CHAPTER 23. MIDDLE RANGES

Make it fun for a change,
Loosen up in the middle range.

Accept a couple of suggestions and write 30-70 words each.
Check out the study hints for this chapter (page 138).

(1)

The baby, given a dose, cries softer by it,
Gets sleepy, conks out, lies quiet.

The Scarlet Letter

The moans of the little patient subsided; its convulsive tossings gradually ceased; and in a few moments, as is the custom of young children after relief from pain, it sank into a profound and dewy slumber. (p. 56)

Describe three steps in waking up.

(2)

In spring the trees don fairness:
Buds and blooms cover bareness.

Their Eyes Were Watching God

She had been spending every minute that she could steal from her chores under that tree for the last three days. That was to say, ever since the first tiny bloom had opened. It had called her to come and gaze on a mystery. From barren brown stems to glistening leaf-buds; from the leaf-buds to snowy virginity of bloom. It stirred her tremendously. (p. 10)

List three stages in the early development of a puppy or kitten.

(3)

In the Ministry of Love
There will come torture!
The state's final shove,
Not maybe...for sure!

Nineteen Eighty-four

It was curious how that predestined horror moved in and out of one's consciousness. There it lay, fixed in future time, preceding death as surely as 99 precedes 100. (p. 116)

Compare the pain preceding report cards to the last two of several numbers.

(4)

Neither extreme uses Slim for George;
The middle will their friendship forge.

Of Mice and Men

If I was bright, if I was even a little bit smart, I'd have my own little place, an' I'd be bringin' in my own crops, 'stead of doin' all the work and not getting what comes up outa the ground." George fell silent. He wanted to talk. Slim neither encouraged nor discouraged him. He just sat back quiet and receptive. (p. 39)

Describe someone listening to a friend or relative starting to ask a favor.

(5)

An idea gives impulse to feeling
And that in stages sends her reeling.

Fahrenheit 451

*"And besides, if Captain Beatty knew about those books - " She thought
about it. Her face grew amazed and then horrified. (p. 79)*

> Describe a happy thought slowing dawning and changing
> a face.

(6)

Happy in her employer's service,
He is making Jane nervous.
If he is to send her away,
Won't that seem like an ice tray?

Jane Eyre

*The thought of Mrs. O'Gall and Bitternut Lodge struck cold to my heart;
and colder the thought of all the brine and foam, destined, as it seemed, to
rush between me and the master at whose side I now walked; and coldest the
remembrance of the wider ocean - wealth, caste, custom intervened between
me and what I naturally and inevitably loved. (p. 282)*

> Compare a situation becoming worse and worse to warm
> water getting hotter and hotter.

(7)

Fisherman, weapon in hand,
Wounds shark biting haul.
Down he sinks as planned:
Large, medium, and small.

The Old Man and the Sea

*The old man settled himself to steer. He did not even watch the big shark
sinking slowly in the water, showing first life-size, then small, then tiny. That
always fascinated the old man. But he did not even watch it now.
(p. 111)*

Describe the large, medium, and small appearance of a
departing bird, plane, vehicle, or person.

(8)

Down falls rain, snow, and hail.
Piano notes descend the scale.
Elevators drop from top to basement.
And so ideas slide to their placement.

Their Eyes Were Watching God

*There is a basin in the mind where words float around on thought and thought
on sound and sight. Then there is a depth of thought untouched by words,
and deeper still a gulf of formless feelings untouched by thought.
(p. 23)*

Describe an idea rising from feeling to thought to words.

(9)

Like a sandwich a thought finds rest.
Not here or there; in-between is best.

Heart of Darkness

He was obeyed, yet he inspired neither love nor fear, nor even respect. He inspired uneasiness. That was it! Uneasiness. Not a definite mistrust - just uneasiness - nothing more. (p. 87)

> Describe something by a word midway between okay and swell.

(10)

Whites to black say hello,
A so-so attitude, you know.

Black Boy

Although I could detect disdain and hatred in their attitudes, they never shouted at me or abused me. It was fairly easy to contemplate the race issue in the shop without reaching those heights of fear that devastated me. (p. 245)

> Describe taunting as falling halfway between two other forms of behavior.

STUDY HINTS

Do your own work. Remember, you have personal ideas to put down and so does everyone else. Above all, do not borrow from a quoted passage.

Before you start, think through these words:

Nouns	Verbs	Adjectives	Adverbs
balance	approach	__,_er,_est	between
decrease	retreat	bordering	first..then
gap	shift	bridging	from..to..
growth	span	broadening	gradually
scale	step	centering	later
spectrum	tend towards	narrowing	nearly
symmetry	waver	not..but..	neither one

While working, turn to dictionaries for exact meanings and search in a synonym dictionary (thesaurus) for better words.

Before reading your finished product aloud, rehearse it until it sounds good. Read the way you talk only a bit slower and louder, remembering to pause between groups of ideas so everyone will "get it."

Begin most sentences low and smoothly raise the pitch to hit each word expressing a new idea. Practice reading this while moving your lips: "The temperature went from morning warm to afternoon boiling, then dropped off to evening chill."

"Good readers make good writers."

CHAPTER 24. KNOWLEDGE AND INSIGHTS

Go "all out" on this your last chance!
What do you know about things like plants?
A final time accept a couple of jobs and write 30-70 words
each. Check out the study hints for this chapter (page 144).

(1)
The leading edge on rabbit stew;
Knowledge from experience grew.

The Grapes of Wrath

He lifted the skin of the back, slit it, put his fingers in the hole, and tore the skin off. It slipped off like a stocking, slipped off the body to the neck, and off the legs to the paws. Joad picked up the knife again and cut off head and feet. (p. 63)

Describe how to perform a manual skill.

(2)
Driving mules according to rules;
Expertise a masterpiece.

Of Mice and Men

He was a jerkline skinner, the prince of the ranch, capable of driving ten, sixteen, even twenty mules with a single line to the leaders. He was capable of killing a fly on the wheeler's butt with a bull whip without touching the mule. (p. 33)

Describe accuracy in driving a car or other vehicle.

(3)

Train travel and camera craft
Carefully described and photographed.
When an author knows the score,
An adventurous tale will not bore.

Orient Express

One thing the films had taught the eye, Savory thought, the beauty of landscape in motion, how a church tower moved behind and above the trees, how it dipped and soared with the uneven human stride, the loveliness of a chimney rising towards a cloud and sinking behind the further cowls. (p. 122)

> Describe what computers have taught us.

(4)

If at home in the land of learning,
Picture academia's overturning.

Brave New World

"You all remember," said the Controller..."that beautiful and inspired saying of Our Ford's: History is bunk..."

He waved his hand; and it was as though, with an invisible feather wisk, he had brushed away a little dust, and that dust was Harappa, was Ur of the Chaldees; some spider-webs, and they were Thebes and Babylon, and Cnossos and Mycenae. Whisk. Whisk - and where was Odysseus, where was Job, where were Jupiter and Gotama and Jesus? (p. 22)

> Describe what would be brushed away if Henry Ford had called another school subject "bunk."

(5)

Nothing is beyond reach,
Whether comic or stern.
Someone must teach,
Someone must learn.

Night

To this day, whenever I hear Beethoven played my eyes close and out of the dark rises the sad, pale face of my Polish friend, as he said farewell on his violin to an audience of dying men. (p. 90)

Describe an artist or dancer saying farewell to everyone at the death camp.

(6)

An author's generosity satisfies our curiosity.

My Antonia

It must have been scarcity of detail in that tawny landscape that made detail so precious. (p. 29)

Describe what is lacking and therefore precious in your city or region.

(7)

Almost never dumb and numb,
Fingers scratch, wave, and drum.

The Keys of the Kingdom

There was an odd tranquillity about his hands. (p.83)

Describe an oddity about arms or legs.

(8)

Power of observation; power of concentration.

Light in August

"Brown was limp. Christmas held his head up, cursing him in a voice level as whispering." (p. 90)

Describe something unusual you've observed about something.

(9)

Show me customs of the sea;
Don't fake it, I'll take it.

Billy Budd

The spot where Claggart stood was the place allotted to the men of lesser grades when seeking some more particular interview either with the officer-of-the-deck or the Captain himself. (p. 59)

Describe a custom of your employer.

(10)

Big ideas in small packages come;
Flash of wisdom always welcome.

One Flew Over the Cuckoo's Nest

Man, when you lose your laugh you lose your footing. (p. 65)

Share an important secret for living that you have discovered.

STUDY HINTS

Do your own work. Remember, you have personal ideas
to put down and so does everyone else. Above all, do not
borrow from a quoted passage.

Before you start, think through these words:

Nouns	Verbs	Adjectives	Adverbs
athlete	cooperate	consistent	ably
baby-sitter	direct	convincing	carefully
gardener	exercise	intelligent	cleverly
musician	explain	patient	forcefully
son/daughter	learn	quick	strongly
student	monitor	skilled	surely
teacher	plant	sympathetic	wisely

While working, turn to dictionaries for exact meanings
and search in a synonym dictionary (thesaurus) for better
words.

Before reading your finished product aloud, rehearse it
until it sounds good. Read the way you talk only a bit slower
and louder, remembering to pause between groups of ideas so
everyone will "get it."

Begin most sentences low and smoothly raise the pitch to
hit each word expressing a new idea. Practice reading this
while moving your lips: "When you lose your laugh, you lose
your footing."

"Good readers make good writers."

ACKNOWLEDGEMENT-BIBLIOGRAPHY-INDEX

I wish to acknowledge the following authors, titles, and publishers for their enormous contribution to this book.

Austen, Jane, Pride and Prejudice (New York:New American Library, 1961). See p. 10.

Bradbury, Ray, Fahrenheit 451 (New York:Random House, 1953). See pp. 16,70,125,131,135.

Bronte, Charlotte, Jane Eyre (New York:World Publishing, 1946). See pp. 4,58,61,65,83,135.

Buck, Pearl S., The Good Earth (New York:Pocket Books, 1958). See pp. 29,109.

Cather, Willa Sibert, My Antonia (New York:Bantam Doubleday Dell Publishing Group, 1994). See pp. 1,26,74,85,106,141.

Conrad, Joseph, Heart of Darkness and The Secret Sharer (New York:New American Library, 1950). See pp. 5,14,39,46,75,113,137.

Conrad, Joseph, Victory (Garden City,N.Y.:Doubleday, 1921). See pp. 79,115.

Cooper, James Fenimore, The Spy (New York:Dodd, Mead, 1946). See pp. 25,82,95.

Crane, Stephen, The Red Badge of Courage (New York:Random House, 1951). See pp. 43,76,103,106.

Cronin, Archibald J., The Keys of the Kingdom (Boston:Little, Brown, 1941). See pp. 55,110,116,119,142.

Dickens, Charles, A Tale of Two Cities (New York:Grosset & Dunlap, 1948). See pp. 16,64,75,93,99,113,127.

Doyle, Arthur Conan, The Complete Sherlock Holmes, Vol. I and II (Garden City,N.Y.:Doubleday, 1927). See pp. 17,61,92,105.

Eliot, George, Silas Marner (New York:Washington Square Press, 1960). See pp. 3,13,23,62,77,86,122.

Faulkner, William, Light in August (New York:Random House, 1950). See pp. 20,21,28,49,53,57,92,97,116,117,129,142.

Fitzgerald, F. Scott, The Great Gatsby (New York:Charles Scribner's Sons, 1925). See pp. 31,38,77,115,127.

145

Golding, William, Lord of the Flies (New York:The Putnam Publishing Group, 1954). See pp. 31,52,111,124.

Greene, Graham, Orient Express (New York:Pocket Books, 1975). See pp. 20,22,22,26,45,52,56,62,69,73,73,123,140.

Hardy, Thomas, The Return of the Native (London:Macmillan, 1952). See pp. 32,35,40,43,46,76,123.

Hawthorne, Nathaniel, The House of Seven Gables (New York:New American Library, 1981). See pp. 40,130.

Hawthorne, Nathaniel, The Scarlet Letter (Philadelphia:Running Press, 1991). See pp. 64,69,83,112,130,133.

Hemingway, Ernest, A Farewell to Arms (New York:Charles Scribner's Sons, 1957). See pp. 47,74,88,121,121.

Hemingway, Ernest, For Whom the Bell Tolls (New York:Charles Scribner's Sons, 1940). See pp. 32,51,53,59,112.

Hemingway, Ernest, The Old Man and the Sea (New York: Charles Scribner's Sons, 1952). See pp. 47,49,97,136.

Hudson, William Henry, Green Mansions (New York:Dodd, Mead, 1949). See pp. 4,27,34,37,37,82,117.

Hurston, Zora Neale, Their Eyes Were Watching God (New York:Perennial Library, 1990). See pp. 34,71,89,133,136.

Huxley, Aldous, Brave New World (New York:Harper & Row, 1946). See pp. 8,50,79,119,140.

Johnson, Samuel, The History of Rasselas, Prince of Abyssinia (London:Penguin Books, 1982). See p. 63.

Kesey, Ken, One Flew Over the Cuckoo's Nest (New York:New American Library, 1962). See pp. 19,28,51,93,143.

Knowles, John, A Separate Peace (New York:Grosset & Dunlap, 1959). See pp. 5,7,25,33,89,124,128.

Lee, Harper, To Kill a Mockingbird (New York:Harper & Row, 1960). See pp. 23,50,67,91,100.

London, Jack, The Sea Wolf (New York:Bantam Books, 1981). See pp. 8,19,68,105,110.

Melville, Herman, Billy Budd (New York:Airmont Publishing Co., 1966). See pp. 1,9,14,35,68,143.

Melville, Herman, <u>Moby Dick</u> (New York:Random House, 1950). See pp. 118,129.

Orwell, George, <u>Animal Farm</u> (New York:Harcourt Brace Jovanovick, 1946). See pp. 11,95,128.

Orwell, George, <u>Nineteen Eighty-four</u> (New York:New American Library, 1961). See pp. 9,44,134.

Paton, Alan, <u>Cry, the Beloved Country</u> (New York:Charles Scribner's Sons, 1948). See pp. 11,13,87,98.

Salinger, J.D., <u>The Catcher in the Rye</u> (Boston:Little, Brown and Co., 1951). See pp. 15,56,80,107,125.

Scott, Sir Walter, <u>Ivanhoe</u> (New York:Washington Square Press, 1980). See pp. 10,29,38,118.

Sinclair, Upton, <u>The Jungle</u> (New York:New American Library, 1980). See pp. 33,71,85,87,100,109,131.

Steinbeck, John, <u>The Grapes of Wrath</u> (New York:Penguin Books, 1967). See pp. 57,63,80,88,103,139.

Steinbeck, John, <u>Of Mice and Men</u> (New York:Penguin Books, 1965). See pp. 7,44,67,104,104,134,139.

Steinbeck, John, <u>The Pearl</u> (New York:The Viking Press, 1947). See pp. 17,27,39,65,98,101,107.

Twain, Mark, <u>The Adventures of Huckleberry Finn</u> (New York:Amsco School Publications, 1972). See pp. 21,91,94,94,111.

Wells, Herbert G., <u>The Time Machine</u> (New York:Berkley Books, 1982). See p. 122.

Wharton, Edith, <u>Ethan Frome</u> (New York:Penguin Books USA, 1987). See pp. 2,2,41,58,59.

Wiesel, Elie, <u>Night</u> (New York:Bantam Books, 1960). See pp. 15,41,45,70,101,141.

Wright, Richard, <u>Black Boy</u> (New York:Harper & Row, 1966). See pp. 3,55,81,81,86,99,137.